NEW EDITION

Geographical Enquiries

Skills and Techniques for Geography

Garrett Nagle & Kris Spencer

Stanley Thornes (Publishers) Ltd

First published in 1997
Second edition published in 2000 by:
Stanley Thornes (Publishers) Ltd
Ellenborough House
Wellington Street
CHELTENHAM GL50 1YW
England

00 01 02 03/ 10 9 8 7 6 5 4 3 2 1

A catalogue record for this book is available from the British Library.

First edition ISBN 0-7487-1670-X
Second edition ISBN 0-7487-5318-4

Designed by Janet McCallum

Printed and bound in China

This book is dedicated to
Angela, Rosie, Patrick, Bethany:
and Muriel

Note to the student

The projects described in this book have been tried and tested, but can only be used as a guide for your own Geography project – they are not complete GCSE projects in themselves. You can use them to help you to write up your own project in the same detail, but you also need to follow the guidelines at the beginning of Section 6 on Geographic Investigations. You must not just copy the projects, but you can adapt them to your particular area. If you live in one of the places that has been used you could update the data and collect more information, or you could study some of the alternate hypotheses.

Acknowledgements

The authors would like to thank the following:

Christine Berry, Tess Brown, Cathy James, Sylvia Penzer and Gill Yeomans.

The pupils of St. Edward's School, Oxford, and St. Paul's Girls' School, London. Especially Eleanor Bucks, Davina Hensman and Alison Thomas.

Claudia Harrison for permission to reproduce her work in the graphs in Figure 6.38 on page 98.

The authors and publishers are grateful to the following for permission to use copyright material:

Edward Arnold, Fig. 4.11, page 43; Hodder and Stoughton, Fig. 4.9, page 42; Institute of Biology, Fig. 6.37, page 97 (from the *Journal of Biological Education*, 25 (3), 1991); Dr. D.H. Mills, Fig. 6.36, page 97; Oxford and County Newspapers, Fig. 6.45, page 106; Penguin Books Ltd, Fig. 2.10, page 27; Reed Information Services, Fig. 6.47, page 108.

Oxford and County Newspapers, Photo 1.4, page 19; Satellite Receiving Station, University of Dundee, Figs. 3.5 and 3.7, pages 31 and 33.

All other photographs supplied by Garrett Nagle.

Maps reproduced from Ordnance Survey mapping with the permission of The Controller of Her Majesty's Stationery Office © Crown Copyright (07000U).

Every effort has been made to contact copyright holders. The publishers apologise to anyone whose rights have been overlooked, and will be happy to rectify any errors or omissions.

CONTENTS

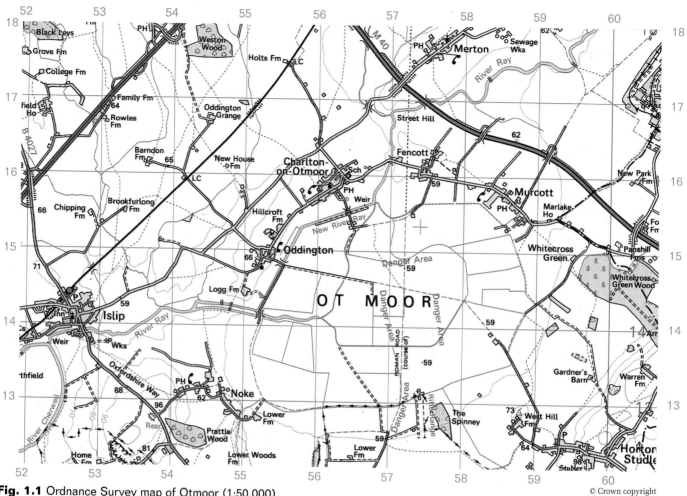

Fig. 1.1 Ordnance Survey map of Otmoor (1:50,000)

© Crown copyright

Most **Ordnance Survey maps** that are used are either at a 1:50,000 or a 1:25,000 **scale**. On a 1:50,000 map 1cm on the map relates to 50,000cm on the ground. On a 1:25,000 map every 1cm on the map refers to 25,000cm on the ground. In every kilometre there are 100,000cm (1,000m x 100cm). Hence:

◆ on a 1:50,000 map every 2cm corresponds to a kilometre

◆ on a 1:25,000 map every 4cm corresponds to a kilometre.

A 1:25,000 map is more detailed than a 1:50,000 map and is therefore an excellent source for geographical enquiries. 1:50,000 maps provide a more general overview of a larger area. You may come across other scales, e.g. 1:10,000 and 1:2,500.

Measurement on maps is made easier by **grid lines**. These are the regular horizontal and vertical lines you can see on an Ordnance Survey map.

The horizontal lines are called **northings** and the vertical lines are called **eastings**. They help to pinpoint the exact location of features on a map.

Questions ▶

1 How many centimetres correspond to a kilometre on:
(**a**) a 1:10,000 map (**b**) a 1:2,500 map?
Which is the more detailed?

2 What colour are the grid lines on:
(**a**) a 1:50,000 map (**b**) 1:25,000 map?

3 To the nearest kilometre, how far is the church at Charlton-on-Otmoor to the church at Islip?

4 To the nearest kilometre, how far is it from the telephone box at Noke to the telephone box at Oddington:
(**a**) by road (**b**) 'as the crow flies'?

GRID REFERENCES & SQUARE REFERENCES

Grid references are the six-figure references which locate precise positions on a map.

◆ The first three figures are the eastings and these tell us how far a position is across the map.

◆ The last three figures are the northings and these tell us how far up the map a position is.

An easy way to remember which way round the numbers go is 'along the corridor and up the stairs'. In Figure 1.1, the Oddington crossing is located at 543158 and the Fencott Bridge is found at 570163.

Sometimes a feature covers an area rather than a point, e.g. all of the villages and the areas of woodland in Figure 1.1. Here a grid reference is inappropriate so we use four-figure **square references**.

◆ The first two numbers refer to the eastings.

◆ The last two numbers refer to the northings.

The point where the two grid lines meet is the bottom left-hand corner of the square. Thus in Figure 1.1, 5815 identifies the square which contains Murcott, while Oddington is found in square 5514. Some features may occur in two or more squares, e.g. Charlton-on-Otmoor is found in squares 5515, 5615 and 5616.

▶ Direction

Directions can be expressed in two ways:

◆ **compass points**, e.g. south-west

◆ **compass bearings** or **angular directions**, e.g. 45°.

Sixteen compass points are commonly used. Some of these are shown in Figure 1.2.

Compass bearings are more accurate than compass points but can be quite confusing. Compass bearings show variations from **magnetic north**. This is slightly different to the **grid north** on the Ordnance Survey map (which is the way in which the northings go). **True north** is different again – this is the direction of the North Pole.

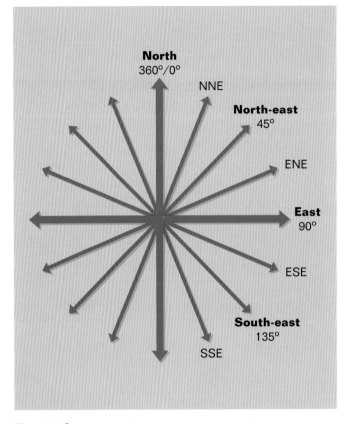

Fig. 1.2 Compass points

Questions ▶

Study the OS map of Otmoor in Figure 1.1.

1 Give the six-figure grid references for:
  (**a**) the bridge over the river at Islip
  (**b**) the sewage works at Merton.

2 What are found at (**a**) 587129 (**b**) 574128?

3 Give the four-figure square reference for
  (**a**) Fencott (**b**) Prattle Wood.

4 What physical features are found at:
  (**a**) 5614 and 5615 (**b**) 6014?

5 Copy and complete Figure 1.2.

Express your answers to the questions below as a compass point and as a compass bearing.

6 What direction is:
  (**a**) Murcott from Charlton-on-Otmoor
  (**b**) Islip from Noke?

7 In what direction does the railway line on the map run?

CONTOURS

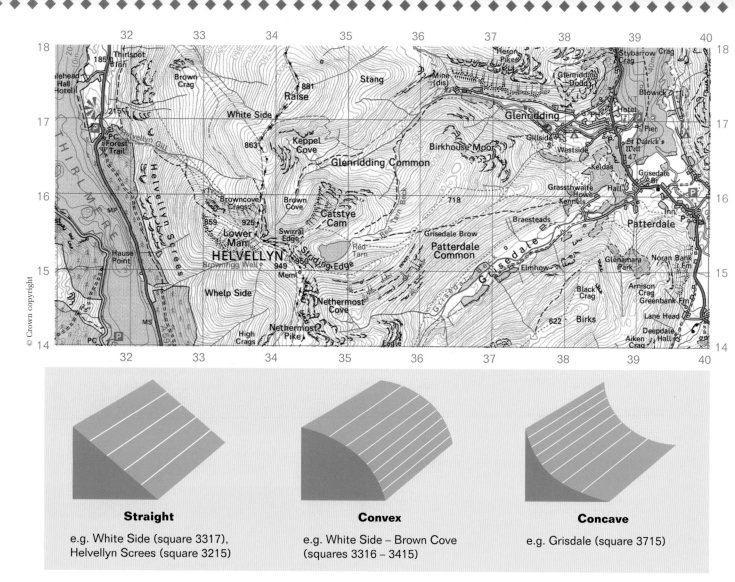

Straight

e.g. White Side (square 3317),
Helvellyn Screes (square 3215)

Convex

e.g. White Side – Brown Cove
(squares 3316 – 3415)

Concave

e.g. Grisdale (square 3715)

Fig. 1.3 Different types of contour lines on Helvellyn

Photo 1.1 Red Tarn and Helvellyn

A **contour line** is a line that joins places of equal height.

◆ When the contour lines are spaced far apart the land is quite flat.

◆ When the contour lines are very close together the land is very steep (when the land is too steep for contour lines a symbol for a cliff is used).

◆ When contour lines are close together at the top, and then get further apart, it suggests a concave slope.

◆ When contour lines are close at the bottom and flat at the top, it suggests a convex slope.

◆ 1 Ordnance Survey maps ◆

GRADIENTS

The **gradient** of a slope is its steepness. We can get a rough idea of the gradient by looking at the contour pattern. If the contour lines are close together the slope is steep, and if they are far apart the land is quite flat. However, these are not very accurate descriptions. To measure gradient accurately we need two measurements:

◆ the vertical difference between two points (this can be worked out using the contour lines or spot heights)

◆ the horizontal distance between two places – this may or may not be a straight line (for example, a meandering stream would not be straight).

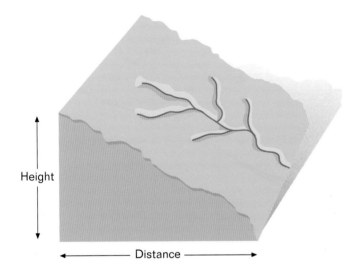

Fig. 1.4 Measuring gradient

▶ Making a cross-section

Make sure that you use the same units for both vertical and horizontal measurements.

Divide the difference in horizontal distance (D) by the height (H). If the answer is, for example, '10' or '5' express it as '1:10' ('one in ten') or '1:5' ('one in five'). This means that for every 10 metres along you rise one metre, or for every five metres in length the land rises (or drops) one metre.

Alternatively, divide the height (H) by the difference in horizontal distance (D) and multiply by 100 per cent (H/D x 100%). This expresses the gradient as a percentage.

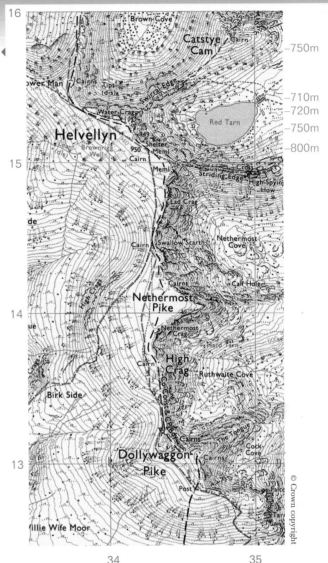

Fig. 1.5 Map extract of Helvellyn

Questions ▶

Study the map extract of Helvellyn in Figures 1.3 and 1.5 and answer the following questions.

1 What is the height of (**a**) Helvellyn (**b**) Red Tarn?

2 What direction does Red Tarn face?

3 How steep is the slope between Helvellyn and Red Tarn? Measure from the peak of Helvellyn to the nearest point of Red Tarn. Express your answer as a percentage and as a 'one in x slope'.

4 Compare the river valleys of Whelp Side Gill (3314) with Grisedale Beck (3614) in Figure 1.3 on page 6. How do you explain the differences?

5 Make a copy of Photo 1.1 on page 6 which shows Red Tarn and Helvellyn. Using information from the map, label (annotate) your sketch to highlight important geographical features.

CROSS-SECTIONS

A **cross-section** is a view of a landscape as it would appear if sliced open, or if you were to walk along it. It shows variations in gradient and the location of important physical and human features. To draw a cross-section:

1 Place the straight edge of a piece of paper between the two end points:

♦ mark off every contour line (in areas where the contours are very close together you could measure every other one)

♦ mark off important geographical features.

2 Align the straight edge of the piece of paper against a horizontal line on graph paper, which is exactly the same length as the line of section:

♦ use a vertical scale of 1cm:100m or 1cm:50m, if you use a smaller scale (e.g. 1cm:10m) you will end up with an slope that looks Himalayan!

♦ mark off with a small dot each of the contours and the geographic factors

♦ join up the dots with a freehand curve

♦ label the features

♦ remember to label the horizontal and vertical scales, title, etc.

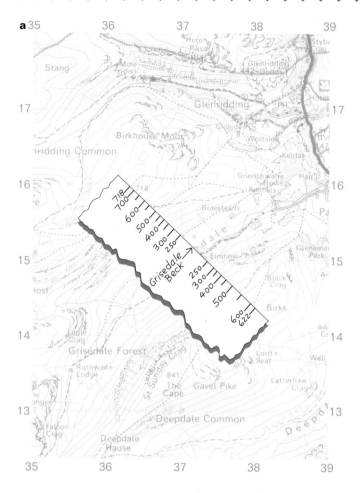

Fig. 1.6 Making a cross-section

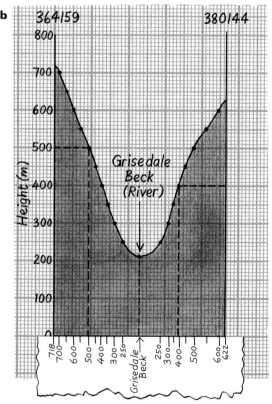

Questions ▶

1 Using the map extract in Figure 1.5 on page 7, draw a cross-section from 350149 (the footpath at the top of Striding Edge), to 345155 (the footpath at the top of Swirral Edge). Label the two arêtes and Red Tarn.
   (**a**) Which slope is the steepest?
   (**b**) Why should this be so?

GLACIAL LANDSCAPES

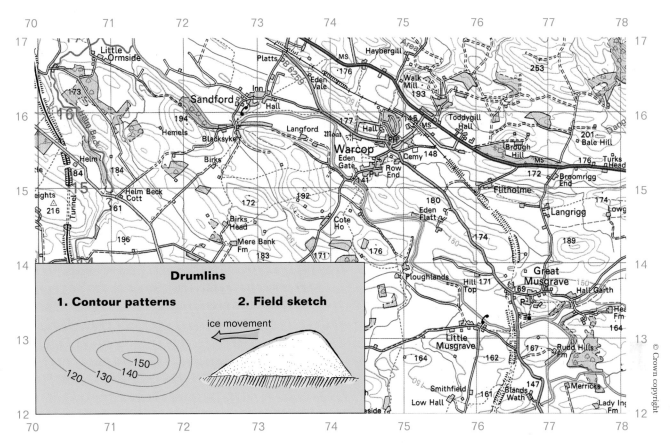

Fig. 1.7 Map extract showing drumlins

▶ Describing a highland region

◆ Where is it located on the map and how much of the map does it cover?

◆ What is the general height of the area (e.g. over 600m, 400m, 250m) and what is the highest point?

◆ What is the shape of the top and the sides: is a plateau with a flat top and steep sides, an escarpment with a steep scarp slope and a gentle dip slope, or is it steep and rugged throughout?

▶ Describing a glaciated highland region

◆ Are the main valleys U-shaped?

◆ Are the tributary valleys hanging valleys?

◆ Do any of the rivers have their source in corries?

◆ Are there any arêtes or pyramidal peaks?

◆ Are there long, narrow ribbon lakes?

▶ Describing a glaciated lowland region

◆ Where are the lowlands and how much of the map do they cover?

◆ What is the general height of the area?

◆ Is it very flat, sloping gently in one direction or undulating?

◆ Is there any evidence of glacial deposition such as moraines, drumlins and eskers? (NB These are very difficult to detect.)

Questions ▶

1 Using the map extracts in Figures 1.3 and 1.7, find a named example, with grid references, of the following features: (**a**) a U-shaped valley, (**b**) a scree slope and (**c**) a drumlin.

2 Describe the relief (topography) of the area in Figure 1.7. Remember to use square references.

3 Using examples from the map in Figure 1.7, show how the natural environment has placed constraints upon human activity.

RIVERS – PHYSICAL GEOGRAPHY

The long profile of a river can be shown on a line graph when the height of a river above base level is plotted against distance from its source. As rivers evolve through time and over distance streams pass through a series of distinct changes. Figure 1.8 shows the long profile of a river and illustrates these stages.

▶ Describing the stage of the river

◆ Is the river in its upper, middle or lower course?

◆ Use the contour lines to describe the shape of the river valley – a V-shaped valley with close contour lines suggests the upper course; more gentle slopes with a broad, flat floodplain suggests the lower course.

◆ Look at the size and shape of the river channel.

◆ Is the channel constrained by relief, i.e. does it flow around interlocking spurs?

◆ Does the river meander across a flat floodplain?

◆ What are the features of the river? Can you identify any of the features listed in Figure 1.8 from map evidence?

Questions ▶

The map extract in Figure 1.9 shows a section of the River Mole south of Leatherhead.

1 Describe the shape of the river's course as it flows from Boxhill Bridge (184503) to Cowslip Farm (164529).

2 Using evidence from the map (remember to give grid references) suggest which stage of the long profile the River Mole is in.

3 Above northing 51 there are no tributary streams flowing into the River Mole. What does this suggest about the geology of the hills to the west and east of the river?

Fig. 1.8 The long profile of a river

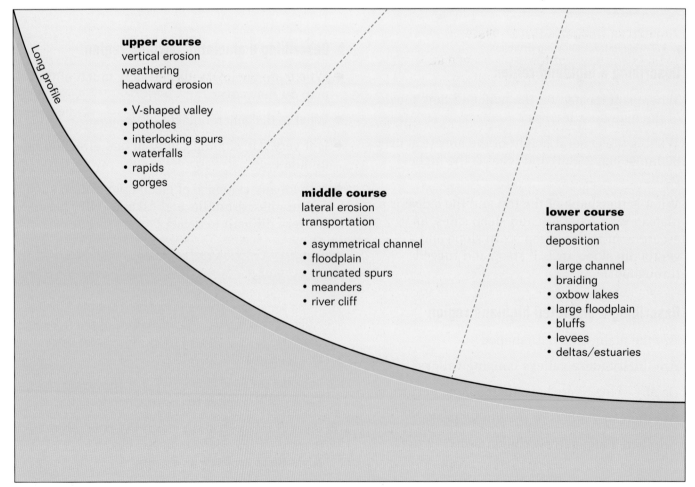

Long profile

upper course
vertical erosion
weathering
headward erosion

• V-shaped valley
• potholes
• interlocking spurs
• waterfalls
• rapids
• gorges

middle course
lateral erosion
transportation

• asymmetrical channel
• floodplain
• truncated spurs
• meanders
• river cliff

lower course
transportation
deposition

• large channel
• braiding
• oxbow lakes
• large floodplain
• bluffs
• levees
• deltas/estuaries

Rivers have had a profound effect on both the site and situation of human settlements. Human activities have also had an increasing impact on drainage basins and river channels. Map evidence can be used to identify the relationship between rivers and human activities.

▶ Describing a river's influence on site and situation

◆ Is the river navigable? (Is it straight and wide enough to allow boats to pass up it?)

◆ Does the river valley provide the only flat land in an area of rough terrain?

◆ Does the valley provide a natural routeway for roads and railway lines?

◆ Do settlements avoid the river's floodplain and locate on higher dry-point sites?

◆ Are settlements located at crossing points on a river? (The name endings of the settlement, such as 'ford' and 'bridge', are evidence of this.)

▶ The human impact on river systems

◆ Is there evidence of forest clearance and wetland reclamation for agriculture?

◆ Does the map show any of the following land-use changes which can affect a river and its drainage basin: mining activity, industrialisation, urbanisation, land drainage schemes?

◆ Has there been any direct interference with rivers through reservoir construction, channel straightening, dams, new channels?

◆ Are there any obvious sources of pollution (industry, sewage works) on the map?

Questions ▶

1 Describe and explain the influence of the River Mole's valley on the major lines of communication shown on the map in Figure 1.9.

2 Draw a sketch map of Westhumble (1651 and 1652) describing the site of this small settlement. Pay particular attention to the influence of the river.

3 There is a sewage works at 176505. What influence might this have on the river ecosystem? (The project described on page 96 will help you.)

Fig. 1.9 Map extract of the River Mole

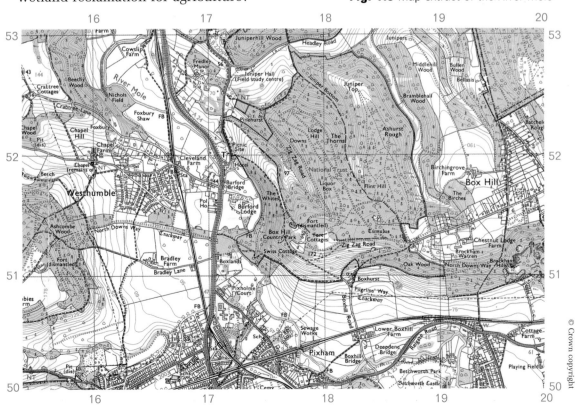

COASTAL LANDSCAPES

▶ Describing coastal scenery

◆ Does the coastline have steep slopes and cliffs suggesting a coastline of erosion? Or are there wide expanses of sand and mud suggesting deposition?

◆ Are there many headlands and bays indicating local changes in processes?

◆ Is the coastline broken by river mouths or estuaries?

◆ What is the direction of the coastline?

◆ Is there any evidence for longshore drift, e.g. spits, bars, tombolos?

◆ Are any of the features named? Give names and grid references.

◆ Is there any map evidence of human attempts to protect the coastline, e.g. groynes, seawalls, breakwaters?

◆ Does the map tell you whether the stretch of coastline is protected or open?

Photo 1.3 Salt marsh

Fig. 1.10 Map extract of Studland

Photo 1.2 Sand dunes

Questions ▶

1 What features do you think are found at 055825? What is the name given to the geographical feature that covers squares 0481, 0581, 0482 and 0582?

2 What type of coastal feature is Studland Heath (0385, 0386)?

3 In what direction do you think longshore drift operates in this area? Give reasons for your choice.

4 Study Photos 1.2 and 1.3 which have contrasting coastlines. One was taken at 024852 and the other was taken at 037861. Identify the geographic features found in each photo. Using the map extract, explain how each feature was formed.

5 Using map evidence give two contrasting pieces of evidence to suggest why erosion is a problem in the area.

6 Using map evidence only, show how people have tried to manage this part of the coastline, i.e. control the processes and features.

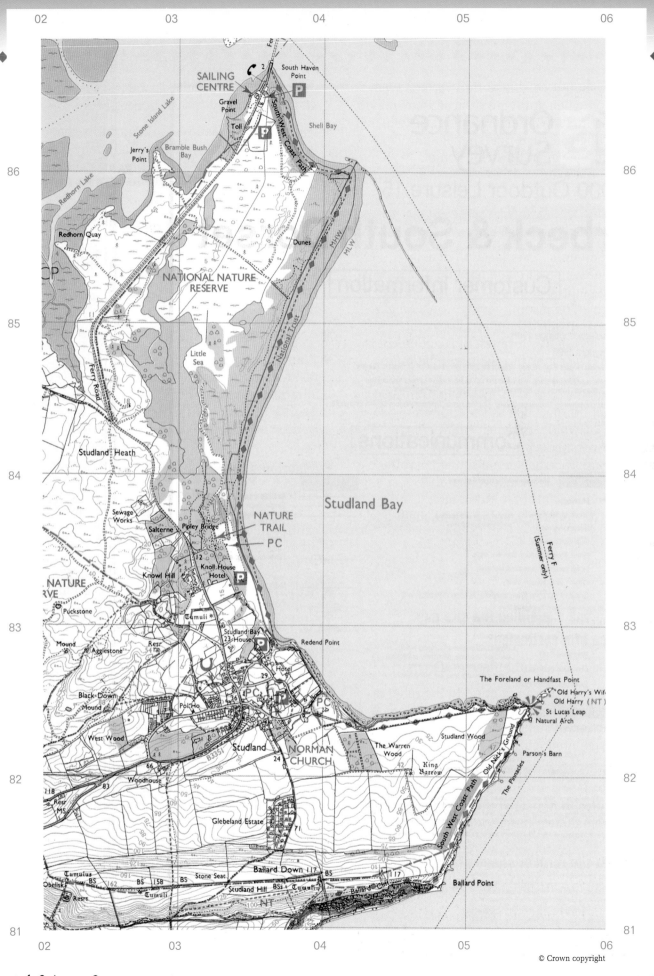

© Crown copyright

RURAL SETTLEMENTS

Geographers should be able to find various types of information when studying rural settlements on a map. These include comments about the site and situation of a village, its form (shape) and function, and the general distribution of settlements on a map.

Definitions	
Site	The immediate location of a settlement, i.e. the land upon which it is built (e.g. on a floodplain, close to a river, on a south-facing slope, on a crossroads, wet point, dry point).
Situation	The relative location of a settlement to a larger area (e.g. Islip in relation to Oxford and Bicester, major routeways such as the M40, and major physical landforms such as the Chilterns, Cotswolds, Thames Valley, etc.).
Function	Any service or employment opportunities that a settlement offers (e.g. commercial, recreational, industrial, agricultural, etc.).
Shape	The appearance of the settlement (e.g. linear, compact, T-shaped).

▶ Describing and explaining the site and importance of a settlement

(see also page 76: central place on Otmoor)

◆ Describe its location in relation to the relief of the area (e.g. valley floor, near or away from a river, direction of slope, dry point, wet point, exposed, sheltered, etc.)

◆ Describe how many routes there are and which forms of transport are available. How important are the routes that meet at the settlement? How does the relief effect these routes?

▶ Describing the form or shape of a settlement

◆ Is it nucleated or dispersed?

◆ Is it a linear or cruciform settlement?

◆ Is any of it modern? (Modern settlement may be recognised by a regular geometric street pattern and more widely-spaced houses.)

◆ Have physical features influenced its shape? (e.g. a steep hillside or floodplain may limit the growth of a town so that it becomes elongated in the direction of the level or dry land.)

▶ Describing the size and function of a settlement

◆ What is the size of the settlement? How many grid squares does it cover? (Each grid square represents 1km².)

◆ Are the houses tightly packed or dispersed?

◆ What functions are evident? For example, residential (housing), commercial (post office, administrative buildings), schools, industry (works, quarries, railway sidings), tourism (tourist information centre, view points).

▶ Describing the situation of a settlement

◆ Using the whole map area, describe the location of the settlement in relation to large urban centres, motorways, 'A' roads, large rivers and other large-scale physical features (such as hills or valleys).

◆ Is the settlement on a rail link? If so, where to?

◆ How accessible is the settlement to motorways, railways and large urban areas? It might be close to a motorway but with no access to it.

▶ Describing and accounting for the general distribution of settlement

(see also page 56: nearest neighbour index)

◆ Locate areas with little or no settlement. Account for lack of settlement in terms of natural disadvantage (e.g. exposed position, steep gradient, flat land in danger of flooding). How is this land used?

◆ Locate areas of fairly close settlement. Account for this in terms of natural advantages for land use and occupation (e.g. farming, water supply, south-facing slope).

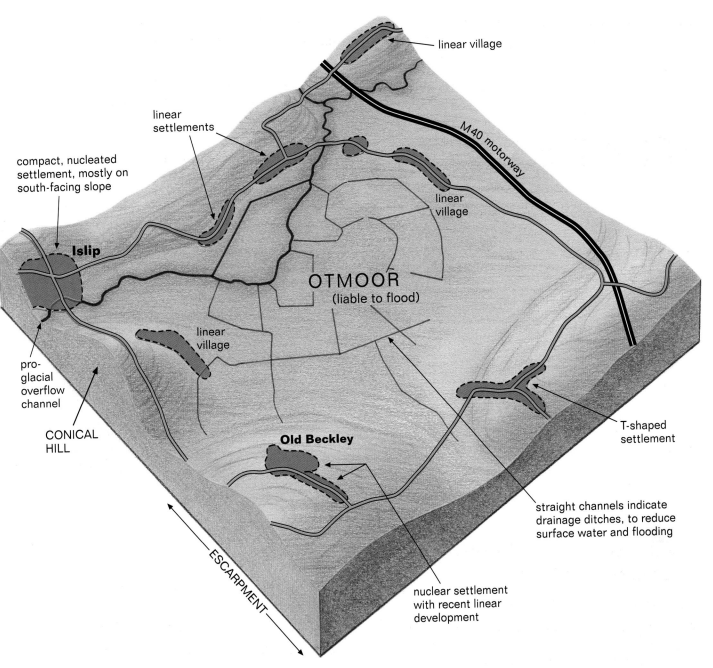

Fig. 1.11 Block diagram showing village shape and site

The following labels appear on the diagram:

- linear village
- linear settlements
- compact, nucleated settlement, mostly on south-facing slope
- **Islip**
- pro-glacial overflow channel
- CONICAL HILL
- linear village
- **Old Beckley**
- ESCARPMENT
- linear village
- M40 motorway
- OTMOOR (liable to flood)
- T-shaped settlement
- straight channels indicate drainage ditches, to reduce surface water and flooding
- nuclear settlement with recent linear development

Questions ▶

Use the extract from the Otmoor region in Oxfordshire in Figure 1.1.

1 Compare the site and situation of Islip (5214) and Horton-cum-Studley (5912 and 6012).

2 Compare the shape of Islip and Horton-cum-Studley. Why do you think they differ?

3 Compare the functions of Islip with those of Noke (5413) and Charlton-on-Otmoor (5615). How and why do they differ?

4 Describe the distribution of settlements in the Otmoor area. How can you explain this pattern?

URBAN AREAS

The Ordnance Survey publishes a range of maps covering urban areas. There are seven major scales:

- ◆ 1:1,250   which covers an area 500m by 500m

- ◆ 1:2,500   which covers an area 1km by 1km

- ◆ 1:10,000   which covers an area 5km by 5km

- ◆ 1:25,000   (Pathfinder) which usually covers 20km east to west, 10km north to south

- ◆ 1:50,000   (Landranger) which covers an area 40km by 40km

- ◆ 1:250,000   (Routemaster) which covers an area 270km by 220km

- ◆ 1:625,000   (Routeplanner) which covers an area 620km by 500km.

The scales 1:1,250, 1:2,500, 1:10,000 and 1:25,000 are shown in this section. The maps represent areas of Port Talbot at different scales.

Questions ▶

1 State and explain which scale of map would be the most useful for each of the following uses.
(a) Planning a route from one part of a town to another.
(b) Planning a route within the same country.
(c) Planning a route from one country to another.
(d) A local area study.

2 As a greater area is shown on a map, some detail is lost. Give three things present on the 1:1,250 and 1:2,500 map extracts of Port Talbot, but not on the 1:25,000. Use grid references to identify the omissions.

3 The most detailed maps are not always the most useful. What advantages does the 1:25,000 map have over the 1:1,250 map?

Fig. 1.12 Port Talbot (1:25,000)

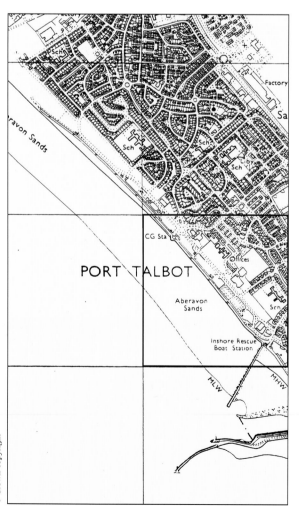

© Crown copyright

Fig. 1.13 Port Talbot (1:10,000)

Crown Copyright 1982

© Crown copyright

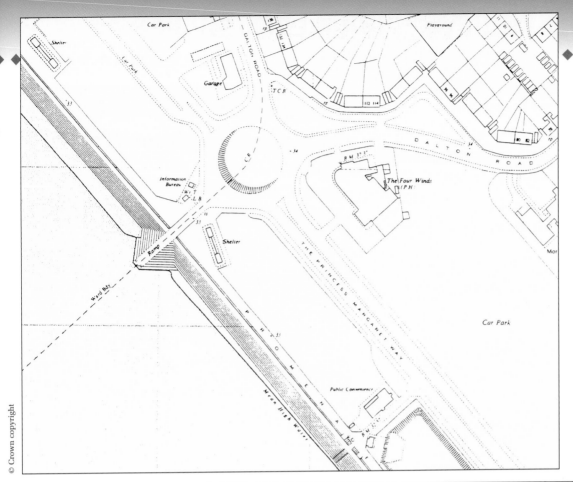

Fig. 1.14 Port Talbot (1:2,500)

Fig. 1.15 Port Talbot (1:1,250)

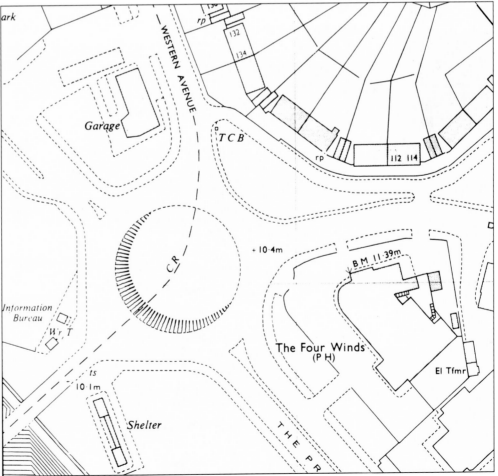

DESCRIBING URBAN LANDSCAPES

It is important to identify different land-use types when describing an urban landscape.

◆ Identify the lines of communication (e.g. roads, railways, airports).

◆ Identify the types of land use (e.g. residential, industrial, commercial). What kind of residential land use is it? Is it terraced, semi-detached, working class, middle class? Is there industry present? If so, what kind? Can you see a CBD or grouping of shops?

◆ If the map is of a whole settlement, can you identify old and new areas?

◆ Use descriptive words when discussing the area: high density/low density housing; regular/haphazard roads; derelict/high-tech industry.

◆ Can you identify any other land uses (e.g. green spaces, derelict land, churches, schools, hospitals)?

Questions ▶

Figure 1.16 is an extract of a 1:10,000 map of Port Talbot.

1 In no more than 250 words, describe the land use of the extract.

2 Now draw a sketch map of the area showing the same information. (NB Remember to simplify your sketch map: try to identify areas of similar function and give them the same shading; annotate your sketch map using descriptive words to identify and explain different land uses.)

3 What are the advantages of using a sketch map to describe urban areas? Are there any disadvantages?

Fig. 1.16 Port Talbot (1:10,000)

© Crown Copyright 1982

INDUSTRIAL LOCATION

The factors determining industrial location are changing. In the first part of this century, heavy industries like iron and steel, ship building and textiles were located close to raw materials or markets. Today, manufacturing industry is drawn to out-of-town or edge-of-town sites. One of the factors is space and another is cost: there is a greater amount of cheaper land available away from the built-up areas of urban areas. Another factor is accessibility: edge-of-town sites are closer to communications (motorways and railways) and the residential workforce who live in suburban areas.

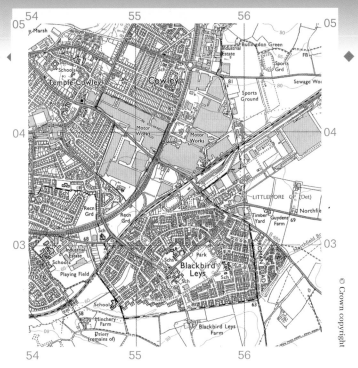

© Crown copyright

Fig. 1.17: Cowley in south Oxford

Questions ▶

Figure 1.17 is an OS map extract of Cowley in South Oxford. The map shows the Cowley motor works. Photo 1.4 is a photograph taken of part of the area.

1 Give three reasons why Cowley is a good site for a car assembly plant.

2 What are the grid references of the following features marked on the photograph?
(**a**) the gasometer marked **A**.
(**b**) Guydens Farm.

3 From what direction was the photograph taken?

4 The photograph shows land which has been cleared from the motor works.
(**a**) Is this shown on the OS map?
(**b**) Suggest two ways in which this land can be used. Explain your choices.

Photo 1.4: The Cowley motor works

A **topological map** distorts real distance and direction in order to achieve a clearer image that is easier to understand. The most famous topological map is Henry C. Beck's diagram of the London Underground. This is what Beck said about his idea:

'Looking at the old map of the underground railways, it occurred to me that it might be possible to tidy it up by straightening the lines, experimenting with diagonals and evening out the distance between stations.'

Figure 2.1 shows a section of Beck's underground map. Figure 2.2 shows what the area looks like in reality. The geographical distortion of the underground map is very great.

Fig. 2.1 London Underground map

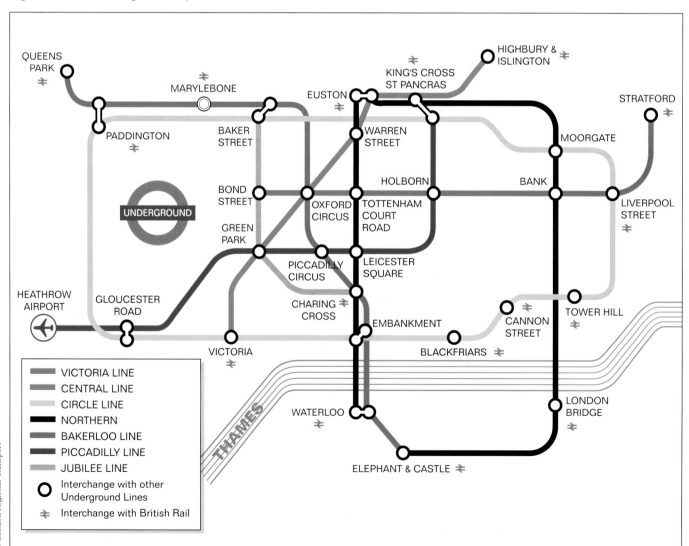

1 Match the names of the stations in Figure 2.1 with the letters of the stations in Figure 2.2.

2 Name the stations which the numbered arrows 1 to 4 lead to.

3 Plan a route from Moorgate to Victoria. Your route should pass through the minimum number of stations possible.

(a) Describe your route giving the names of stations and the lines on which you travel.
(b) How many changes of lines have you made?
(c) What are the disadvantages of a large number of changes?

4 Which of the two maps would be the more useful if you wanted to:

(a) visit the Houses of Parliament from Victoria station?
(b) plan a sightseeing trip to include London Bridge, Piccadilly Circus and Baker Street?

5 Figure 2.2 has a scale. Suggest why Figure 2.1 has no scale.

Fig. 2.2 Scale map

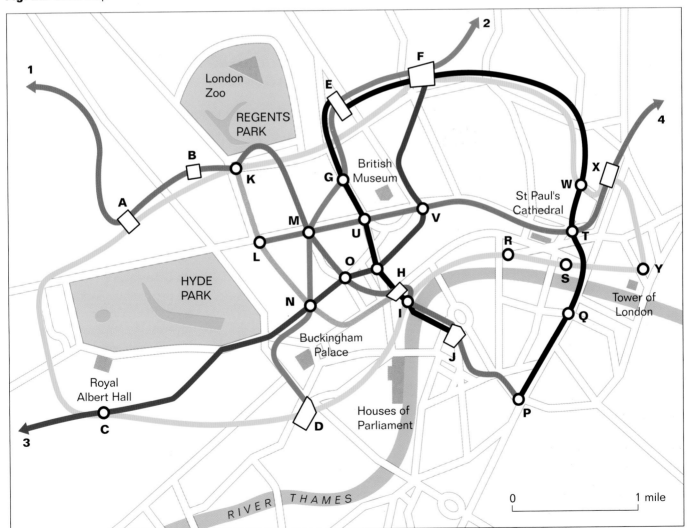

GEOLOGICAL MAPS

Geological maps tell us about the underlying bedrock. When we know the main rock types it helps us to understand the landscapes.

For example, even if we know about a rock's permeability and its hardness we can make a four fold classification (see Figure 2.4).

◆ **Permeability** refers to a rocks ability to transmit water: a permeable rock, such as chalk or limestone, allows water to pass through and is usually dry on the surface. By contrast, an impermeable rock, such as clay or granite, holds water and will normally have rivers, streams or marshland on the surface.

◆ Hard rocks (such as granite and limestone) form upland areas with steep slopes; whereas soft rocks (such as clay, sands and gravels) form lowland areas, usually with gentle or undulating slopes.

The simplified geological map and cross-section of the Isle of Purbeck (in the bottom right-hand corner of Figure 2.3) shows that there is a wide variety of rocks in a very small area. The Ordnance Survey extract shows the area covered by the cross-section.

The geological sketch map in Figure 2.3 shows a part of the coastline in more detail.

Photo 2.1 Durdle Door

Fig. 2.3 Geological sketch map

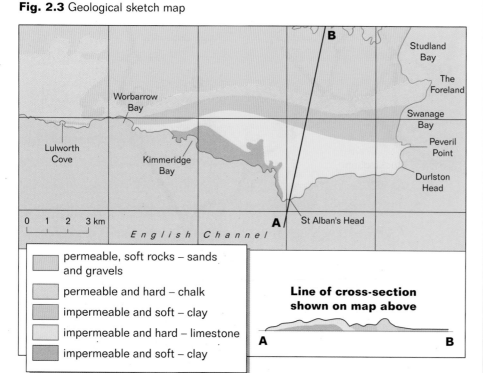

Studland Bay
The Foreland
Worbarrow Bay
Swanage Bay
Lulworth Cove
Peveril Point
Kimmeridge Bay
Durlston Head
St Alban's Head
0 1 2 3 km
English Channel
A
B

- permeable, soft rocks – sands and gravels
- permeable and hard – chalk
- impermeable and soft – clay
- impermeable and hard – limestone
- impermeable and soft – clay

Line of cross-section shown on map above
A   B

Questions ▶

1 Look at Photo 2.1 of Durdle Door.

(**a**) What coastal features are shown at points **1**, **2** and **3**?
(**b**) The rock types on the photograph are **A**: chalk, **B**: clay and **C**: limestone.
  (**i**) Explain how rock types have affected the formation of the features in the photograph.
  (**ii**) What evidence is there to suggest that area **A** is chalk from the OS map (in Figure 2.5)?

2 How do rock types influence landforms? Use specific examples to illustrate your answer from Figures 2.3 and 2.6, and Photo 2.2 of Corfe Castle.

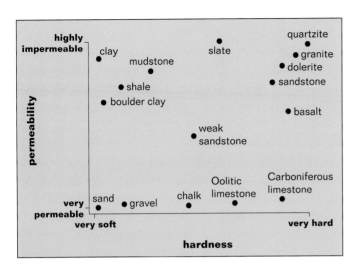

Fig. 2.4 Rock type, permeability and hardness

Photo 2.2 Site of Corfe Castle

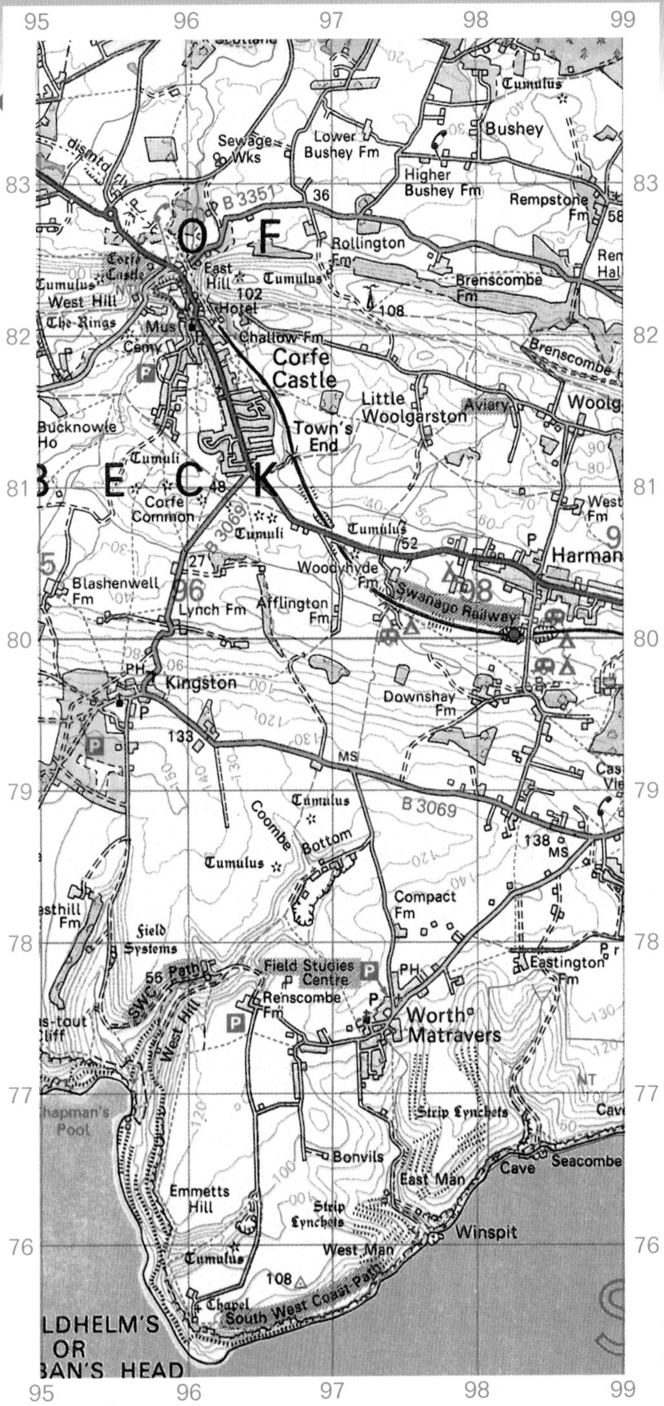

Fig. 2.6 Map extract showing cross-section area

Fig. 2.5 Map extract of Lulworth Cove (1:25,000)

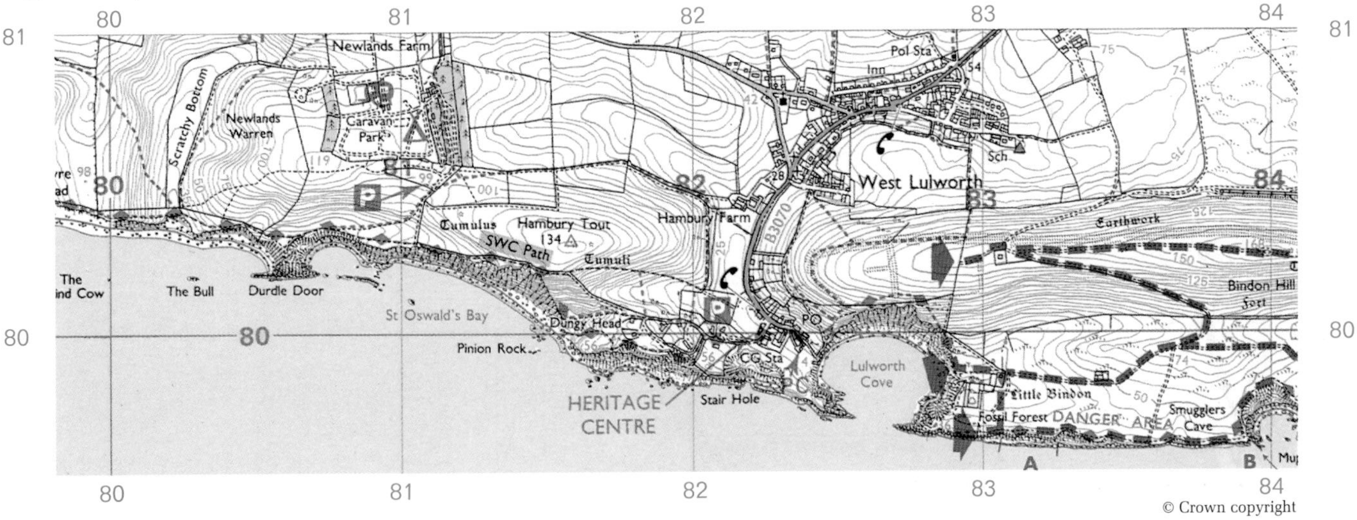

© Crown copyright

© Crown copyright

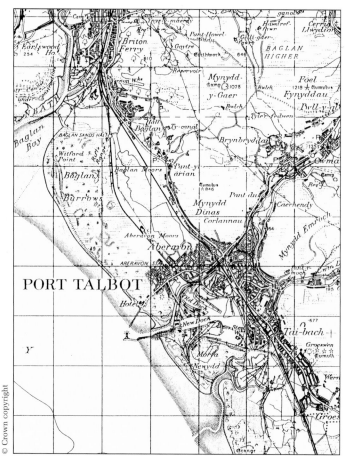

Fig. 2.7 Port Talbot (1952)

Fig. 2.8 Port Talbot (1923)

Fig. 2.9 Aberavon (1888)

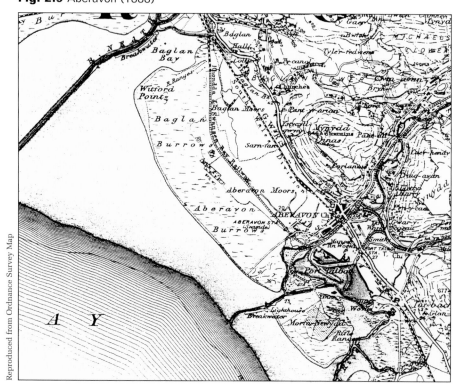

Questions ▶

Look carefully at the maps on this page.

1 In 1888, which settlement is most important, Aberavon or Port Talbot? Explain your answer.

2 Use all the map extracts to describe the growth of Port Talbot from 1888 to 1952.

3 Port Talbot is close to the coalfields of South Wales and is used for the import and export of raw materials and finished steel for a large steel works at Llanwern. How do you think these factors have affected its growth?

MENTAL MAPS

Geographers are interested in measuring the images that people have of places. Human beings, both in groups and as individuals, prefer some places to others. We may have detailed knowledge of our local environment but know very little about another area which is more distant. Factors like age, sex, social class and experience affect our perception of places. We filter out some aspects of our environment and concentrate on others.

One way of studying the way people perceive the world is through **mental maps**. Each person has a unique mental map of the world at a variety of scales, but certain groups may share viewpoints. We can study individual mental maps or we can combine a number of viewpoints (see Figure 2.10).

Questions ▶

1 One way of generating a mental map is by asking a study group (which could be your class) to draw or describe their journey to a certain place; it could be a school or famous landmark.

(a) Describe your journey to school using an annotated sketch map. Scale is not important, but some sense of direction should be given.
(b) Which of the following landmarks are mentioned most often in your description: buildings; shops; green areas; residential areas?
(c) Why do you think some landmarks are more memorable than others?

2 Figure 2.10 shows the responses of a number of school leavers when asked 'Where would you like to live?' The resulting isolines record preferences. The higher the number on the isoline, the more the respondents in each group wanted to live there.
(a) Account for the differences and similarities between the mental maps of school leavers at Redcar, Bristol and Inverness.
(b) Why might the maps be useful to the following interest groups:
    (i) a firm interested in building starter homes?
    (ii) local tourist boards?
    (iii) a foreign firm looking to locate in the UK?
(c) How far do you share the viewpoints expressed on the maps?

Fig. 2.10 Mental maps of school leavers when asked 'Where would you like to live?' (From *Mental Maps*, P. Gould and R. White, Penguin)

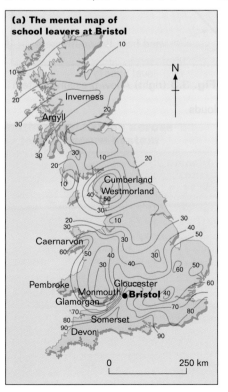

(a) The mental map of school leavers at Bristol

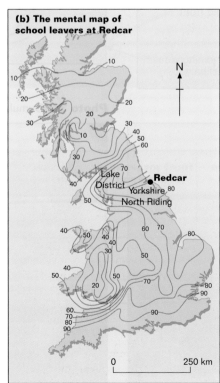

(b) The mental map of school leavers at Redcar

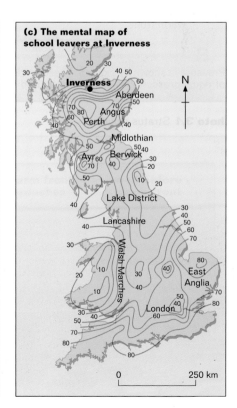

(c) The mental map of school leavers at Inverness

WEATHER SATELLITES & LOW PRESSURE SYSTEMS

The weather map and the satellite image show a low pressure system (or depression) centred off the south coast of Iceland. The satellite was taken at 1639 GMT on the 30th March 1994 and the weather map shows the situation at noon on the same day.

The weather forecast for the day stated that:

'...most places will start cloudy with rain in places. More general rain will spread from the west. Scotland and Ireland will remain cloudy and wet. The rain will become more persistent. The rain will clear by 31st March and conditions will get brighter with scattered showers. Some showers may be quite heavy.'

Questions ▶

1 Describe how the low pressure system **A** (shown on the weather map) appears on the satellite map.

2 What is the difference between the isobars (the isobar interval) on the map?

3 What is the pressure of the system **A**?

4 How do you explain the changes in temperature between the far north of Scotland and northern England?

5 Why is the eastern side of Ireland covered in cloud, whereas the western side is largely clear?

6 How do satellite images help us to predict the weather? State two ways.

7 What are the limitations of using satellite images? State two ways.

Fig. 3.4 Weather map showing a low pressure system

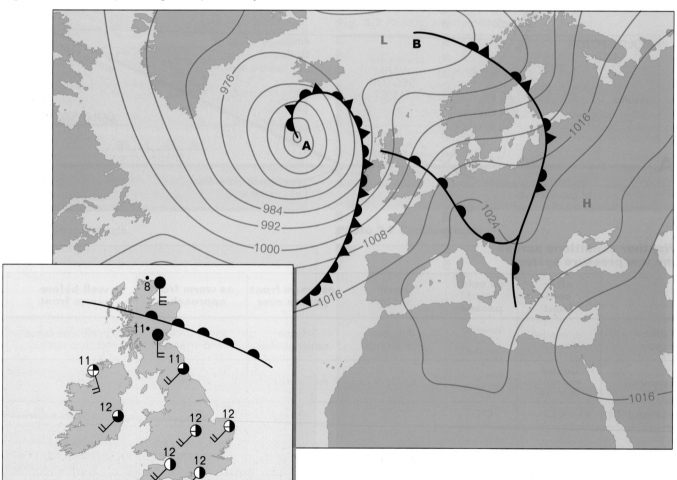

Fig. 3.5 Satellite image of a low pressure system

HIGH PRESSURE SYSTEMS

High pressure systems (or anticyclones) act very differently compared with low pressure systems (or depressions).

◆ Low pressure systems produce wet, windy weather.

◆ High pressure systems produce hot, sunny, dry calm days in summer; and cold, sharp, crisp days in winter. (Winter nights are cold as sparse cloud cover allows heat to escape. Frost and fog are also common in winter and autumn.)

Winds in a high pressure system blow out from the centre of high pressure in a clockwise direction (compared with a low pressure system where they blow into the centre of low pressure in an anti-clockwise direction). The winds are light, hence the isobars on a high pressure weather chart are circular and spaced far apart.

Figure 3.6 shows a weather map for a high pressure system. The weather forecast for the day stated:

'...a slow moving anticyclone will dominate the British Isles for the next few days. Most places will be dry and sunny. Northern Scotland and the Northern Isles will have some coastal fog patches.'

Fig. 3.6 Weather map showing a high pressure system

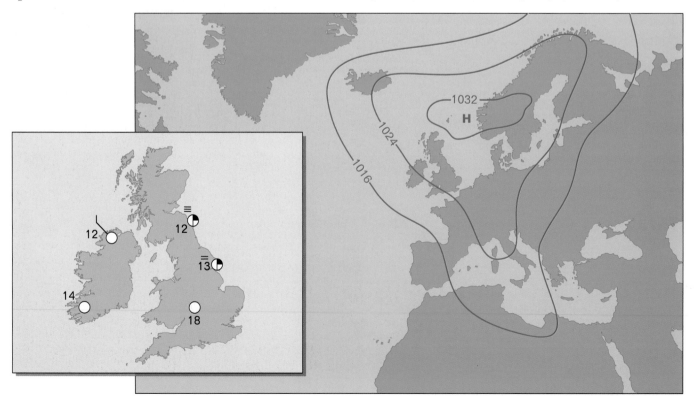

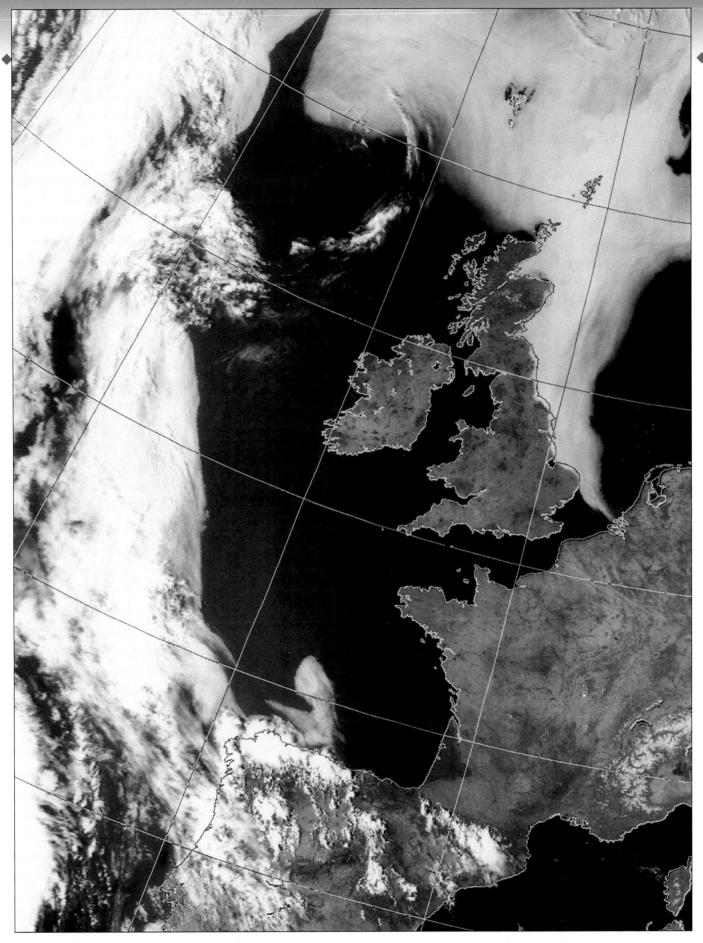

Fig. 3.7 Satellite image of a high pressure system

CLIMATIC GRAPHS

Simple **climatic graphs** (or climographs) tell us a great deal about the seasonal pattern of rainfall and temperature. More detailed climographs help us to see variations within the monthly pattern.

There is a contrast between the climographs of a mountainous area such as the Lake District, with that of a lowland region such as Oxford.

In Figure 3.8 we can see how the **mean monthly average** occurs between the **mean monthly maximum** and the **mean monthly minimum**. (The mean monthly maximum is the average of all the maximum temperatures for each day of the month, and the mean monthly minimum is an average of all the minimum temperatures recorded for that month.) We could also show the **absolute maximum** and the **absolute minimum** for that month, although the climograph begins to look cluttered. The rainfall is generally shown as a bar chart. Different scales are normally used to show temperature and rainfall: in this example the temperature scale is shown on the left-hand side and the rainfall scale is shown on the right-hand side. We can show how the weather pattern varies at a particular place by comparing climographs of different years.

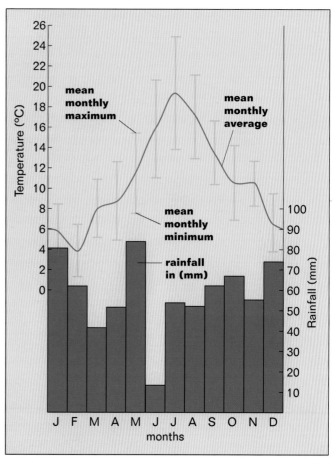

Fig. 3.8 Climatic graph for Oxford, 1994

Fig. 3.9 Climatic data for Oxford, 1990

1990	Jan	Feb	Mar	Apr	May	Jun	Jul	Aug	Sep	Oct	Nov	Dec	Year
Mean temp. (°C)	7·1	8	8·5	8·1	13·2	14·3	17·7	19	13·6	12·3	6·8	4·3	11·1
Mean max. temp. (°C)	10	11·3	12·7	13·7	19	18·2	23·8	24·8	18·6	15·8	9·8	7	15·4
Mean min. temp. (°C)	4·5	5·2	5	3·2	7·9	10·7	12·2	14	9·4	9·3	4·2	1·7	7·3
Rainfall (mm)	75	94·2	18·4	20·4	8·7	48·4	17·7	26·5	41·1	45·9	20	56·3	473

Questions ▶

1 Plot the climatic data in Figure 3.9 for Oxford in 1990 (the same station as shown in Figure 3.8). The data was recorded in an exceptionally hot year which had a long lasting drought.

2 From the graph you have drawn, answer the following questions.
(**a**) Which part(s) of the year 1990 suffered the most drought? Give reasons for your choice.
(**b**) In which months do you think the temperature was above average? (Use the data for Oxford in Figure 3.9 to help you.)
(**c**) How does (**i**) the annual temperature pattern and (**ii**) the annual rainfall pattern that you drew differ from those in Figure 3.8?

3 How predictable is the weather for a particular area? Explain your answer.

4 What are the implications of the variations in the annual weather patterns for (**a**) farmers and (**b**) water resources?

FLOOD HYDROGRAPHS

A **flood hydrograph** shows how a storm affects a stream or river over a short period (such a few hours or up to a few days). Flood hydrographs show a number of features as follows, these vary from stream to stream.

◆ **Discharge** is the amount (volume) of water passing a point over a given length of time, i.e. litres per second or metres per second (cumecs).

◆ **Peak flow** marks the greatest discharge of the stream.

◆ **Time lag** is the difference in time between the peak of the storm and the peak of the flood.

◆ The **rising limb** is the rising floodwater, whereas the **recessional limb** is the declining floodwater.

◆ **Base flow** is the normal flow of the river, i.e. water that passes through rocks to reach the river.

◆ **Storm flow** (or quickflow) is the rapid flow that the storm creates. It usually flows over the surface to the stream, hence it arrives quickly.

Questions ▶

1 Plot the following figures on to graph paper. They were derived for the same storm as in Figure 3.11, but from a nearby urban stream.

Fig. 3.10 Urban stream

Time (min)	Discharge (l/sec)
0	2·2
30	4·0
60	10·0
90	17·5
120	22·0
150	18·0
180	13·0
210	9·2
240	7·0
270	4·8
300	3·7
330	3·2
360	2·9
390	2·8
420	2·0

(**a**) What is the peak flow and time lag in your urban hydrograph?

(**b**) How do the rising limb and recessional limbs in the new hydrograph compare with the original (rural) one in Figure 3.11?

(**c**) Explain these differences with reference to the increase in impermeable surfaces (e.g. pavements, roads, buildings) and number of drainage channels (e.g. sewers, gutters, drains, ditches, streams).

Fig. 3.11 A model storm hydrograph

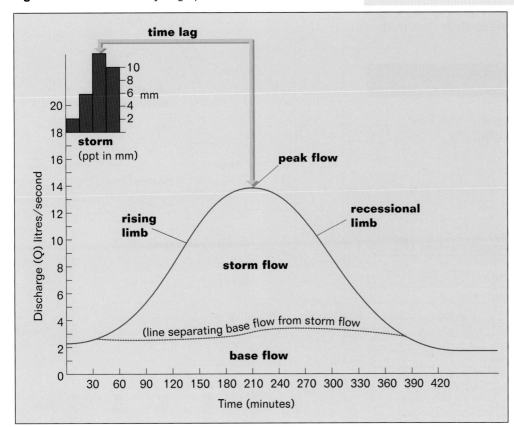

4 Graphical representation

LINE GRAPHS

Line graphs are quite simple graphs which show continuous changes over time. For example, a line graph which shows population change between 1951 and 1991, can show changes for 1951–52, 1952–53, 1953–54 and so on. They use **continuous data** and they show **trends**. These changes can be **absolute** or **relative**. Line graphs can be **simple** (showing one feature) or **multiple** (showing many trends).

In all line graphs there are independent and dependent variables. For example, the rainfall figures for St. Edward's School, Oxford are shown in Figure 4.1. The year is the independent variable, and rainfall is the dependent variable. The independent variable is plotted on the horizontal (or *x* axis) and the dependent variable is plotted on the vertical (or the *y* axis). It is important to label the axes and to show the scale clearly. It is possible to add the **average**, **trend** or the **inter-quartile range (IQR)** to the line graph. This aids in the description of the graph. (For an explanation of the IQR see page 52.)

Multiple line graphs (as in Figure 4.2) show the variation in many features, for example, changes in the water quality of a stream above and below a sewage outlet. If there is an overlap then the use of different colours or different symbols is required.

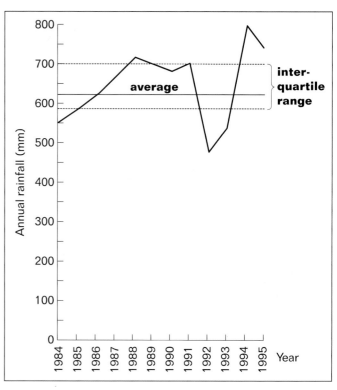

Fig. 4.1 Rainfall in Oxford (1984–95)

Fig. 4.2 A multiple line graph showing agricultural yields

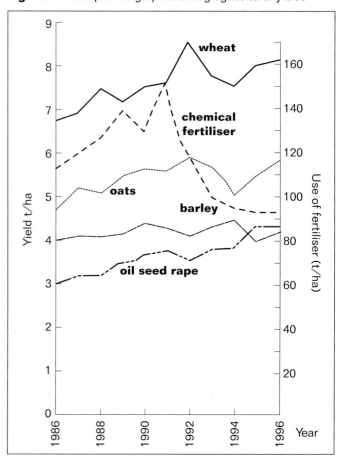

Questions ▶

1 Construct a line graph from the following data which shows variations in water quality along a stream. You will have to use different scales for water temperature and oxygen content. The distance between each site is 50m. There is a sewage outlet at site 4 and a weir at site 5.

Site	Temperature (°C)	Oxygen content (%)
1	18·0	0·12
2	17·8	0·14
3	17·8	0·12
4	21·3	0·11
5	21·6	1·84
6	22·4	1·71
7	21·4	1·33
8	22·0	1·54
9	21·7	1·45
10	21·5	1·60

SCATTERGRAPHS

Scattergraphs show how two sets of data are related to each other (e.g. population size and number of services, or distance from the source of a river and average pebble size). They are often used alongside **Spearman's rank correlation coefficient** (see page 52) which tests to see if there is a statistical relationship between two sets of data.

To plot a scattergraph, decide which variable is independent (in Figure 4.3 it is organic content, or distance from the source) and which is dependent (number of services or average pebble size). The independent is plotted on the horizontal or *x* axis and the dependent on the vertical or *y* axis. A dot or cross is marked where the *x* and *y* values for each site meet on the graph (see example A on Figure 4.3, where the projected lines are drawn in from the *x* and *y* axes).

Questions ▶

1 Construct a scattergraph using the following data.

Site	Discharge (m³/sec)	Suspended load (g/m³)
1	0·45	10·8
2	0·42	9·7
3	0·51	11·2
4	0·55	11·3
5	0·68	12·5
6	0·75	12·8
7	0·89	13·0
8	0·76	12·7
9	0·96	13·0
10	1·26	17·4

When all the data are plotted, draw a line of best fit. This does *not* have to pass through the origin. It is useful to label some of the points (e.g. largest and smallest, anomalies [exceptions]) especially if these are referred to in any later description.

Fig. 4.3 A scattergraph of the relationship between organic content and moisture content of soils

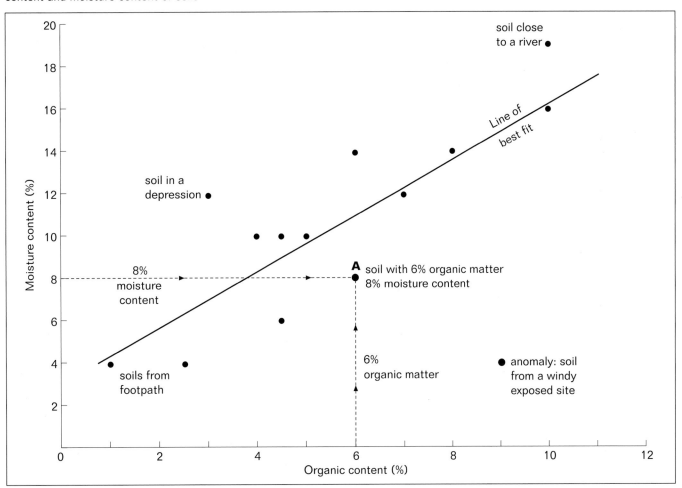

PIE CHARTS

◆◆◆

Pie charts and **proportional pie charts** are frequently used on maps to show variations in size and composition of a geographic feature. In Figure 4.4 the size of the pie chart varies with the amount of crime, and the divisions within the pie chart vary with the type of crime.

▶ Plotting the pie chart

Every 3·6° on the pie chart represents 1% of the circle. To plot values, first convert them into percentages and then multiply by 3·6. This gives the number of degrees that will make up each segment (e.g. 36° for 10%, 90° for 25% and so on).

1 The following data shows rates of crime in three selected areas of Oxford, namely Wolvercote (**W**), Blackbird Leys (**BL**) and the city centre (**CC**).

	BL	W	CC
Shoplifting	1	0	474
Robbery	18	0	22
Burglary	223	17	112
Car theft	365	53	39
Sexual	7	0	4
Total	614	70	651

2 Putting this data into percentages we get:

	BL	W	CC
Shoplifting	0·2	0·0	72·8
Robbery	2·9	0·0	3·4
Burglary	36·3	24·2	17·2
Car theft	59·4	75·8	6·0
Sexual	1·1	0·0	0·6
Total	100	100	100

3 These percentages are then multiplied by 3·6 and rounded to the nearest whole number, to give us the number of degrees that each segment will be:

	BL	W	CC
Shoplifting	1	0	262
Robbery	10	0	12
Burglary	131	87	62
Car theft	214	273	22
Sexual	4	0	2
Total	360	360	360

▶ Determining the size of circle

The size (or area) of the circle has to be proportional to the value it represents to draw **proportional pie charts**. The area of a circle is found by using the formula πr^2, therefore the circles are drawn in relation to the square root of the value.

1 Decide on the largest size of circle to be used on your map (in this example, 3cm). Write down its radius (r) (in the case of Figure 4.4 it is 3cm).

2 Work out the square root of all values that will be mapped.

3 Using the square root of the largest value to be mapped (in this example 25·5), work out the value (V) that it will be multiplied by in order to make the actual circle on the map (in this example, 0·12). Now multiply all the other values by this figure.

Value	Square root	V	Radius of circle (r)
651	25·5	0·12	3·0
614	24·8	0·12	3·0
70	8·4	0·12	1·0

▶ Advantages

Proportional pie charts can show a wide range of data and show geographic variations. They are a very striking visual technique. The main disadvantage is that it overemphasises large figures and therefore small figures are not as clear. They also require time, care and patience to draw.

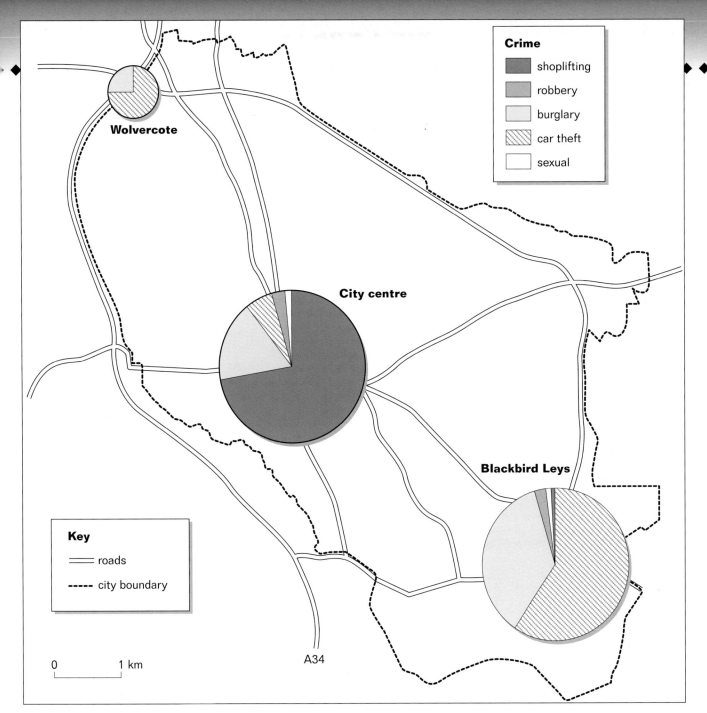

Fig. 4.4 Proportional pie charts showing the rate and type of crime

	Footpath 1	Footpath 2
Walkers	8	27
Joggers	1	3
Horseriding	0	2
Cyclists	0	4

1 Draw two proportional pie charts to show the number and type of people using each of the footpaths, one heavily used and the other less heavily used.

2 From the results you have drawn, identify which is the more heavily-used footpath and which is the less heavily-used footpath. Describe how the type of use varies between them.

BAR CHARTS

In **bar charts** the length of each bar represents the quantity of each component (e.g. places or time intervals). The vertical axis has a scale which measures the total of each of these components. There are four main types of bar chart, as follows.

◆ **Simple bar chart**: each bar indicates a single factor. If the difference in length of the bars is not great, then differences can be emphasised by leaving a space between them or by 'breaking' the vertical scale.

◆ **Multiple or group bar chart**: features are grouped together on one graph to help comparison.

◆ **Compound or component bar chart**: various elements or factors are grouped together on one bar (the most stable element or factor is placed at the bottom of the bar to avoid disturbance).

◆ **Percentage compound or component bar chart**: this is a variation on the compound bar chart, it is used to compare features by showing the percentage contribution. These graphs do not give a total in each category, but compare relative changes in percentages.

Fig. 4.5a Ethnic origin in Glasgow compared with GB base

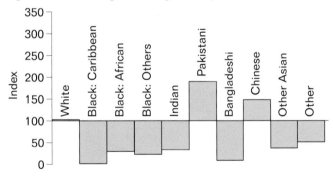

Questions ▶

Figures 4.5a, 4.5b and 4.6 show a variety of 1991 census data about Glasgow.

1 What kind of bar charts are Figures 4.5a, 4.5b and 4.6?

2 Figure 4.5a shows data about Glasgow's ethnic population. The index figure of 100 is Great Britain's average for each group.
(**a**) What do the bars beneath the 100 index line represent?
(**b**) What is the dominant ethnic group in Glasgow?

3 Figure 4.5b is a percentage compound graph.
(**a**) Which of the following statements can be supported by the map?
◆ Manchester has a greater total of ethnic minorities than Glasgow.
◆ Edinburgh has the lowest population of ethnic minorities in its total population.
(**b**) Explain your answer.

Fig. 4.5b Ethnic minorities in Glasgow compared with GB base and other cities

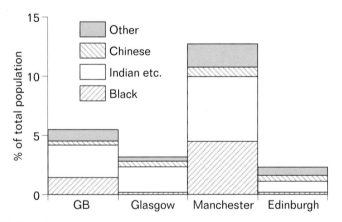

Fig. 4.6 Population pyramids are an interesting variation on multiple bar charts

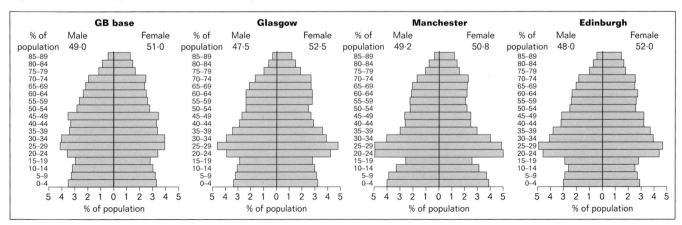

◆ **4 Graphical representation** ◆

PICTOGRAMS

Pictograms (or picture graphs) are an interesting way of presenting data. In a pictogram, a picture or symbol is used to represent the data. The number of times a symbol occurs can represent the value or amount – in this way the pictograms act very much like a bar chart (see Figure 4.5). Another method is to show the value by increasing or decreasing the size of the symbol.

Questions ▶

1 Figure 4.7 shows the type of goods a sample of shoppers bought in Hammersmith's CBD.
(**a**) Why are people more likely to buy groceries rather than electronic goods?
(**b**) How many people purchased clothes and shoes?
(**c**) Redraw the pictogram using only one symbol for each type of good. Develop a scale so that the size of symbol represents the total shoppers.
(**d**) Compare your pictogram with Figure 4.7. Which pictogram is the most successful? Give reasons for your answer.

2 How successful is Figure 4.8 in conveying its message?

Fig. 4.7 What do you purchase in Hammersmith?

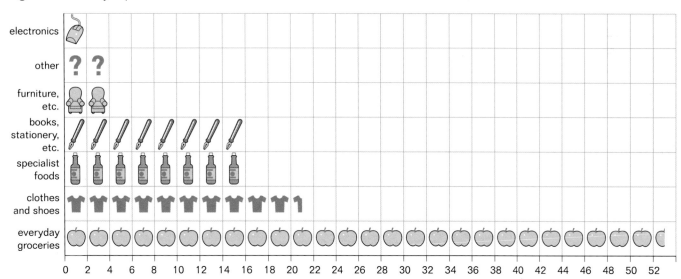

Fig. 4.8 Do you find shopping areas crowded and congested?

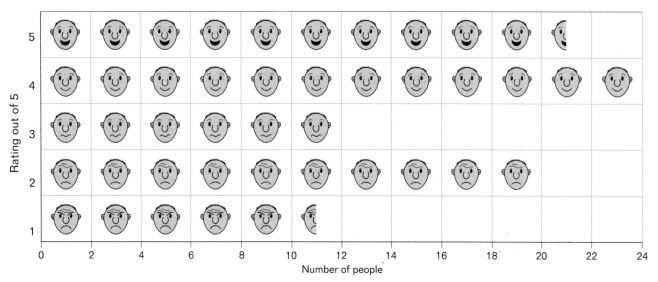

FLOW-LINE MAPS

Flow-line maps show the volume of movement between places. Direction is indicated by an arrow. The quantity or volume is shown by varying the thickness of the line. A number of guidelines should be followed:

◆ the map must have a key

◆ the range of thickness must be carefully selected (the lines should identify large and small flows without cluttering or obscuring detail)

◆ the background map must be kept as simple as possible (sometimes it is best just to put the place names on the map or even use a plain background).

Questions ▶

Figure 4.9 shows a flow-line map of traffic in a suburb to the north of Bolton, a town in Lancashire.

1 (a) What was the traffic flow at all the points marked **A** through to **I**?
(b) Explain the greater traffic volumes at **D** than at **C** and **E**.

2 Explain how the information displayed on Figure 4.9 might be useful to:
(a) a commuter.
(b) a town planner.
(c) a person wishing to buy a house in the area.

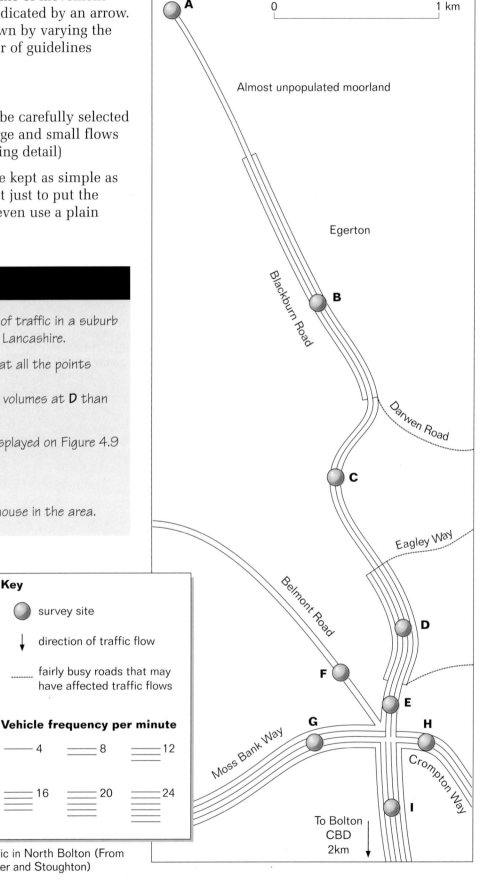

Key

⬤ survey site

↓ direction of traffic flow

------ fairly busy roads that may have affected traffic flows

Vehicle frequency per minute

—— 4   ═══ 8   ═══ 12

═══ 16   ═══ 20   ═══ 24

Fig. 4.9 (right) Flow-line map of traffic in North Bolton (From *Practical Photography*, K. Briggs, Hodder and Stoughton)

ISOLINE MAPS

An **isoline** is a line which joins places of equal value or amounts. **Isoline maps** are used when we have data from a number of study points in an area. Drawing isolines allows the data to be used to describe the whole study area rather than a series of points. Examples of isolines commonly used in geography are:

◆ **contour lines** which join points of equal height

◆ **isobars** which join points of equal air pressure

◆ **isotherms** which join points of equal temperature

◆ **isohyets** which join points of equal precipitation.

▶ Constructing an isoline map

The first thing to remember is that it is not just a matter of joining the dots. Choose isolines which increase regularly (e.g. every 10, 25 or 100, depending on the data spread). The more data points you have, the more accurate the map will be. You then need to estimate the position of your isoline relative to each point.

Fig. 4.10 Contour lines in metres

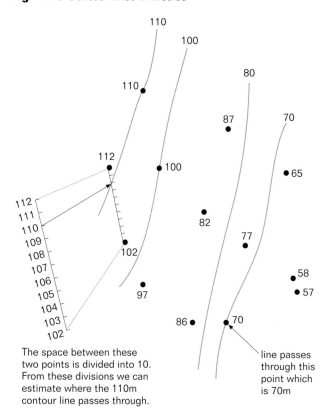

The space between these two points is divided into 10. From these divisions we can estimate where the 110m contour line passes through.

line passes through this point which is 70m

Questions ▶

1 Figure 4.10 shows a simplified map of heights above sea level. It has been annotated to show how isolines are constructed.
   (**a**) Trace Figure 4.10 into your book and draw in the 90m and 60m contour lines.
   (**b**) What would it mean if the contour lines were closer together?

2 Figure 4.11 shows isolines representing the deposition of oxides of sulphur between 1880 and 1991 in Europe.
   (**a**) Use an atlas to locate the regions with the highest totals.
   (**b**) Why is the monitoring of this kind of pollution so important?
   (**c**) Explain the different isoline values over Europe.

Fig. 4.11 Total deposition of oxidised sulphur in Europe (1880–1991) (From *The Global Casino*, N. Middleton, Edward Arnold)

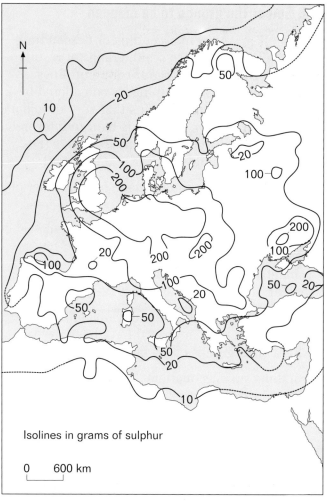

Isolines in grams of sulphur

0   600 km

CHOROPLETHS

A **choropleth** is a map which shows relative density per area. This includes percentages, ratios and per capita information (such as average income). Choropleths are easy to construct and provide a striking visual impact of the data, e.g. the rates of crime in Oxford (page 105) or agricultural inputs per field (see Figure 4.12).

However, there are important limitations to bear in mind. Choropleths are based on areas and suggest that conditions are constant within an area. They also suggest sharp contrasts at the boundaries of areas, which is not necessarily true.

To draw a choropleth three tasks must be carried out as follows.

▶ 1. Collect and produce the data to be mapped

In Figure 4.12 the data has already been collected from the farmer, hence this stage has been done (i.e. the values have been produced).

▶ 2. Select the groups to be mapped

The data is arranged in ascending or descending order. This allows you to see the range of results and also if there are any significant groupings. Between four and six groupings is considered best: less than four groupings means that very little data is shown, while more than six is hard to interpret. Groupings must also be mutually exclusive (i.e. any one value can only appear in one group).

Groupings or classes can be made on a number of intervals:

- ◆ **arithmetic intervals** where the groups change at a constant rate (e.g. 0–4, 5–9, 10–14)

- ◆ **geometric rates** where the classes change by a regular ratio (e.g. 1–2, 3–4, 5–8, 9–16)

- ◆ **natural breaks** if there are obvious groups (e.g. the rates of crime in Oxford have been derived where clear groups could be chosen)

- ◆ **fractions** such as quarters, fifths or sixths (i.e. there is a similar number of observations in each group).

▶ 3. Choose an appropriate shading to draw the map

Shading should be done in one colour. In some cases two colours can be used effectively. Areas with the highest values should be darkest and those with the lowest values should be lightest. This emphasises the importance of the greater intensity. If there are more than two colours it becomes difficult to tell which colour (and therefore area) is the most important.

Questions ▶

The following data show wheat yields (tonnes/ha) for the fields shown in Figure 4.12. Make a copy of the blank field pattern in Figure 4.12 and choose an appropriate scale to show the data in not more than four groups.

A	6·8
B	7·2
C	4·5
D	5·6
E	7·3
F	3·1
G	4·4
H	5·9
I	6·7
J	6·5
K	4·5
L	6·0

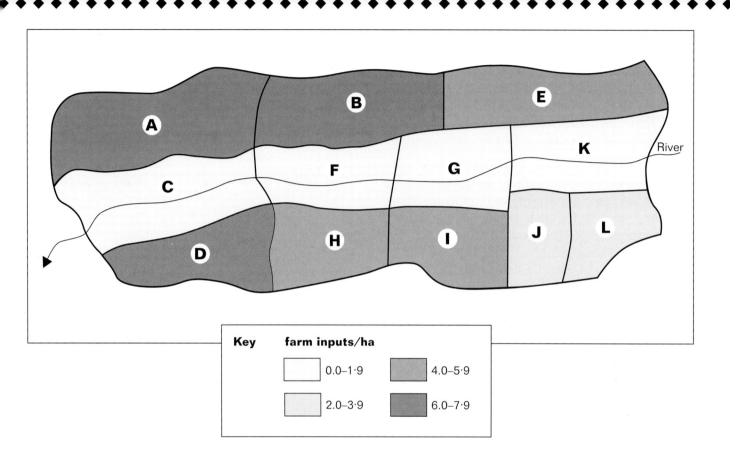

Key **farm inputs/ha**

0.0–1·9

2.0–3·9

4.0–5·9

6.0–7·9

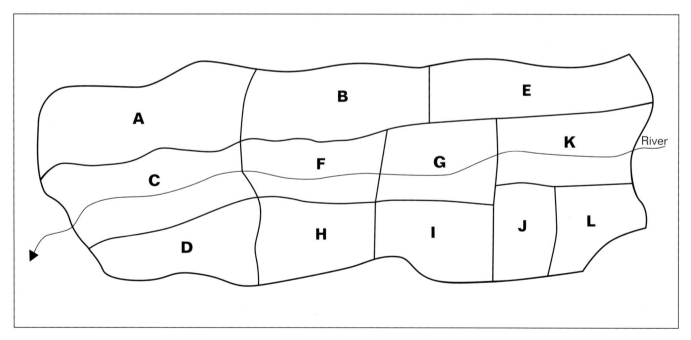

Fig. 4.12 Agricultural yields (top) per field (farm inputs/ha)

DISPERSION DIAGRAMS

A **dispersion diagram** is a very useful diagram for showing the range of a set of data, their tendency to group or disperse, and also for comparing two sets of data. It is rather like a bar chart on its side, with frequency on one axis and groupings on the other. Dispersion diagrams can also be successfully used to determine the class intervals for choropleths.

The following dispersion diagrams in Figure 4.13 show the percentage covering of lichens on east-facing and west-facing gravestones on a graveyard in Cassington, Oxon. It is possible to compare the two diagrams to see whether there is any difference in the amount of lichen cover.

Questions ▶

1 Look at the following data on pebble size from an upper course site and a lower course site of a river in the Lake District.

	Pebble size (mm)
Upper course	32, 45, 21, 34, 48, 23, 24, 37, 43, 27, 56, 46, 37, 32, 45, 51, 20, 43, 38, 36, 26, 45, 19, 40, 46, 32, 56, 39, 30, 43
Lower course	23, 12, 17, 26, 10, 9, 25, 31, 25, 30, 16, 19, 12, 19, 22, 13, 25, 9, 12, 31, 26, 18, 23, 31, 20, 12, 16, 27, 18, 23

(**a**) Draw two dispersion diagrams, using the same scale on each, to show whether there is any difference between the size of pebbles in an upper course river and a lower course river.
(**b**) How useful do you think the method is for portraying this data? Support your answer with examples.

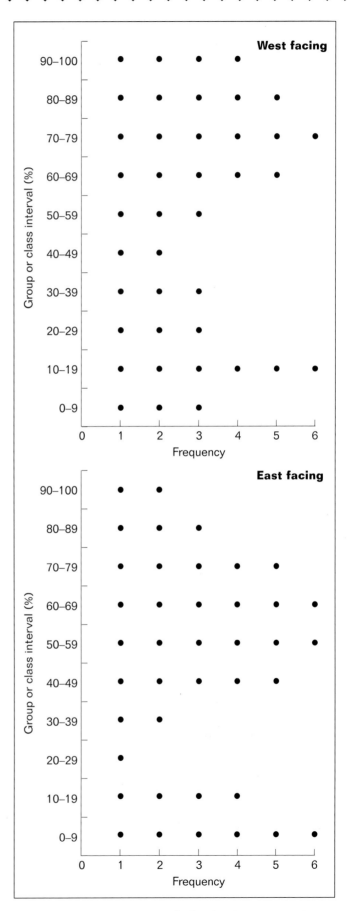

Fig. 4.13 (right) Dispersion diagrams to show the percentage of lichen cover on east-facing and west-facing gravestones

TRIANGULAR GRAPHS

Triangular graphs are used to show data that can be divided into three parts. This includes soil (sand, silt and clay), employment (primary, secondary and tertiary), and population (young, adult and elderly). Figure 4.14 shows a triangular graph for soil textural classes. The data must be in the form of a percentage and the percentage must total 100 per cent. The main advantages of triangular graphs are that:

◆ a large number of data can be shown on one graph (many pie charts or bar charts would be used to show all the data on Figure 4.14)

◆ groupings are easily recognisable (e.g. in the case of soils, groups of soil texture can be identified)

◆ dominant characteristics can be shown

◆ classifications can be drawn up.

Triangular graphs can be difficult to interpret and it is easy to get confused, especially if care is not taken; however, they provide a fast and reliable way of classifying large amounts of data which have three components.

Questions ▶

Look at Figure 4.14.

1 Identify the following soils: **A**, **B**, **C**, and **D**.

2 Trace the triangular graph in Figure 4.14 and plot the following:
   (**a**) clay 30%, sand 45% and silt 25%.
   (**b**) clay 50%, sand 30% and silt 20%.
   (**c**) clay 20%, sand 35% and silt 45%.
   (**d**) clay 37%, sand 36% and silt 27%.

Fig. 4.14 Triangular graph of soil textural classes

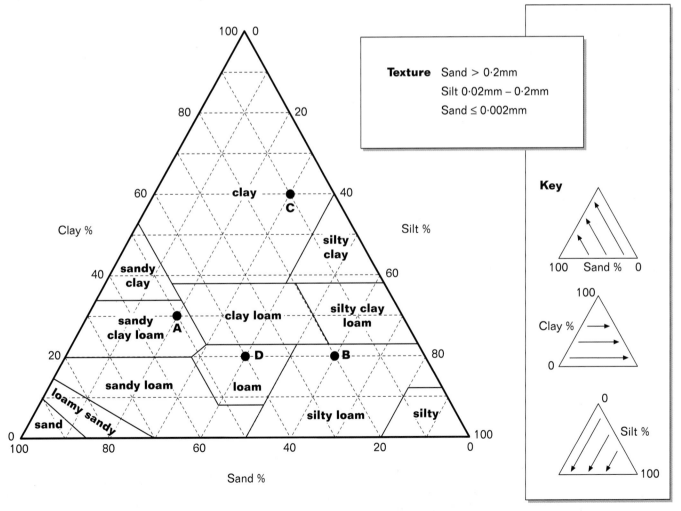

Texture   Sand > 0·2mm
Silt 0·02mm – 0·2mm
Sand ≤ 0·002mm

ANNOTATED SKETCH DIAGRAMS & PHOTOGRAPHS

Photo 4.1 Durdle Door

It is important that you label (annotate) sketch diagrams clearly to show all the important features. You may wish to use secondary material to help you in this, such as geology, type of soil, slope angle, village size, etc.

Many photographs that are used in examinations are aerial views which show industrial, residential, recreation and commercial land-uses. In your projects you are likely to have much simpler photos. However, if you use your photos carefully you can show a number of interesting and valuable features.

Fig. 4.15 Coastal landforms at Durdle Door, Dorset

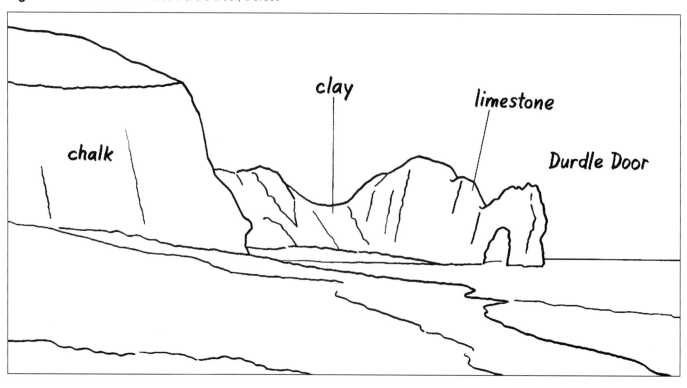

Photo 4.2 Urban landscape near St Pancras, London

Questions ▶

1 Copy and complete the sketch diagram in Figure 4.15 of Durdle Door. Your labels should include arch, cliff, wave-cut platform, grassland vegetation, low wave energy (clear skies, high pressure producing low wind speeds) and sea at low tide.

2 Make an annotated diagram of Red Tarn shown in the Photo 1.1 on page 6. Labels for Red Tarn include Red Tarn, Helvellyn, Swirral Edge, frost shattered slopes, steep slopes, north-east facing and Red Tarn Beck.

3 Look carefully at Photo 4.2. State two features about traffic restrictions in the area.

4 Describe the type of housing:
(a) how many storeys are there?

(b) what does the photo tell us about the amount of garden space?
(c) are the houses likely to be owned or rented and how can you tell?

5 What are the buildings made of? How old are the buildings?

6 What type of buildings and land uses can you see in the photo?

7 Where in the city would you expect to find this area (CBD, inner city area, suburbs, etc.)?

8 Using all this information, draw an outline of the area in the photograph and annotate it.

There are many types of **statistics**, some of them extremely easy and some very complex. At the most basic there are simple **descriptive** statistics. These include the:

◆ **mean** or average

◆ **maximum** (largest) and **minimum** (smallest)

◆ **range** which is the maximum minus the minimum

◆ **mode** which is the most frequently occurring number, group or class

◆ **median** which is the middle value when all the numbers are placed in ascending or descending rank order.

In any project or enquiry it is important to use descriptive statistics – they provide invaluable summaries of the data and are often the only statistics that are appropriate.

There are four different types of data ('data' are plural, 'datum' is singular), as follows.

◆ **Nominal data** refer to objects which have names (e.g. rock types, land uses, dates of floods, famines) – these are the most basic type of data. For example, in a Geographic Investigation we might categorise settlements as being hamlets, villages or towns, and then count them to form a hierarchy. Alternatively, when studying urban functions we may classify areas as being industrial, commercial, residential, recreational and so on (these may later be expressed as percentages of total land use.)

◆ **Ordinal** or **ranked data** refer to objects when they are placed in ascending or descending order (e.g. London, Birmingham and Manchester would be ranked 1, 2 and 3 in terms of their population sizes, although we do not have to know their exact sizes). Settlement hierarchies are often expressed in terms of ranks. One of the most commonly-used statistics in Geography is Spearman's rank correlation coefficient, which compares two sets of ranked data (e.g. population size and number of services, or pebble size and distance from source) to test whether they are related.

◆ **Interval data** and **ratio data** refer to real numbers. – Interval data is different from ratio data. In

interval data there is no true zero. This means that if Oxford has a mean temperature of 13°C and Miami 26°C, it is not possible to state that Miami is twice as warm as Oxford: for if we had used degrees Fahrenheit, the figures would have been about 59°F and 79°F degrees respectively. – Ratio data possess a true zero. For example, it is possible to have 0mm rainfall, or 0kg crop yield, and so it is possible to say that Miami with about 2000mm of rainfall is about three times as wet as Oxford, which has about 670mm per year.

The simplest data – nominal – can only yield quite simple, albeit important information, whereas more complex data can be tested with more complex statistics.

Questions ▶

1 What types of data are the following:
(**a**) 16°C, 18°C, 30°C, -2°C
(**b**) 250mm, 4mm, 16mm, 0mm
(**c**) Drought, flood, famine, earthquake
(**d**) 1st, 2nd, equal 3rd, equal 3rd, 5th, 6th?

One of the most commonly-used statistics is the **mean** (or average). This is found by totalling the values for all observations ($\sum x$) and then dividing by the total number of observations (n): $\frac{\sum x}{n}$

For example, the number of services in eight villages was found to be: 3, 10, 4, 6, 1, 4, 2, 6. The average is:

$$\frac{3+10+4+6+1+4+2+6}{8} = \frac{36}{8} = 4{\cdot}5$$

Obviously, there cannot be half a service (except where there are mobile shops or post offices that only open for limited periods of time), so the mean is not always the best statistic to use.

The **mode** refers to the group or class which occurs most often. In this case both '4' and '6' occur twice and these are the **modal groups**. A pattern which has two peaks, as in this case, is called **bimodal**. One clear peak is known as **unimodal**.

Another method is to use the **median**. This is the middle value when all the data are placed in ascending or descending order (e.g. in this case 10,

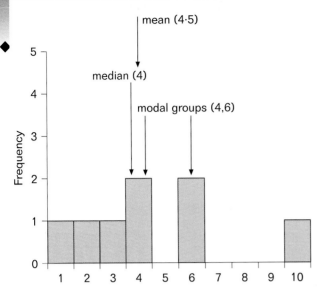

Fig. 5.1 Graph showing mean, median and modal groups

6, 6, 4, 4, 3, 2, 1). When there are *two* middle values we take the average of these (e.g. in this case it is quite simple because both are 4, hence the median is 4).

▶ Summarising groups of data

Sometimes the data we collect is in the form of a group. For example, slope angles (or ages) may be recorded as: 0–4, 5–9, 10–14, 15–19, etc.

Finding the mean in this case is slightly more difficult. We use the mid-point of the group and multiply this by the frequency.

Slope angle (°)	Mid-point	Frequency (f)	Mid point x frequency
0–4	2	6	12
5–9	7	12	84
10–14	12	7	84
15–19	17	5	85
20–24	22	0	0
Total		$n=30$	$\Sigma fx=265$

Mean $= \dfrac{\Sigma fx}{n} = \dfrac{265}{30} = \mathbf{8 \cdot 81}°$

The modal group is the one which occurs with the most frequency, e.g. 5–9°. The median (or middle value) will be the average of the 15th and 16th values when ranked: these are both in the 5–9° group.

1 The following rainfall measurements (in mm) were recorded over a one week period: 4, 2, 1, 7, 5, 0, 2.
(**a**) Plot the data on a graph similar to Figure 5.1.
(**b**) Work out the mean, the mode and the median.
(**c**) Which of these descriptive statistics best summarises the data for these figures? Which is least satisfactory? Justify your choice.

2 A survey of distances travelled by shoppers to a hypermarket is shown below.

Distance (km)	Number of shoppers
0–2	16
3–5	23
6–10	12
11–15	8
16–20	1

(**a**) Plot the data in the form of a bar graph.
(**b**) Work out the mean, modal group and median distance travelled by shoppers to the hypermarket.
(**c**) Which of these measures is:
　　(**i**) most satisfactory　(**ii**) least satisfactory?
Explain your choice.

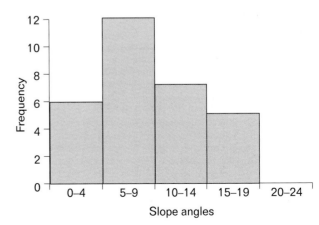

Fig. 5.2 Frequency of slope angles

▶ Measures of dispersion

So far we have looked only at ways of summarising the data by showing some sort of 'average'. This is sometimes referred to as a **measure of central tendency**, giving one figure to describe a complete data set. It is often just as useful to show how far figures differ from the average. This is known as **dispersion**, and there are a number of ways of showing this.

The simplest way to show dispersion is to use the **range** – the difference between the maximum (largest) and the minimum (smallest) values. This has its limits and is limited on data where there is considerable variation between the records, as in the case of rainfall figures for example.

An alternative measure is the **inter-quartile range**. This is similar to the range, but only gives the range of the middle half of the results – by this the extremes are omitted, the importance of which is clearly illustrated in Figure 5.3. If we put the rainfall figures in order from Figure 5.3 we get: 75, 80, 84, 86, 125, 148, 184, 192, 195, 209, 235, 274, 361, 361, 390, 418, 452, 460, 538, 807.
The **maximum** is 807mm, the **minimum** is 75mm,

and the **range** is thus from 807mm to 75mm, i.e. 732mm.

The **inter-quartile range** is found by removing the top and bottom **quartiles** (quarters) and stating the range that remains. The first quartile is termed Q_1 and the third quartile Q_3. The interquartile range is $Q_1 - Q_3$. In the example in Figure 5.3 this is quite easy, as we take the 5th value (Q_1) from the 15th value (Q_3): 75, 80, 84, 86, 125, 148, 184, 192, 195, 209, 235, 274, 361, 361, 390, 418, 452, 460, 538, 807. Thus the inter-quartile range is $390 - 125 = 265$, a reading which clearly gets rid of the extremes.

Fig. 5.5 Dispersion diagram of rainfall figures for Tel Aviv (1973–93)

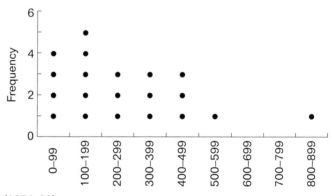

Fig. 5.3 Rainfall figures for Tel Aviv (mm) over a 20-year period

Year	Rainfall (mm)
1974	86
1975	125
1976	184
1977	75
1978	538
1979	192
1980	418
1981	80
1982	361
1983	460
1984	807
1985	361
1986	209
1987	452
1988	235
1989	195
1990	274
1991	148
1992	390
1993	84

Fig. 5.4 Rainfall for Tel Aviv (1974–93)

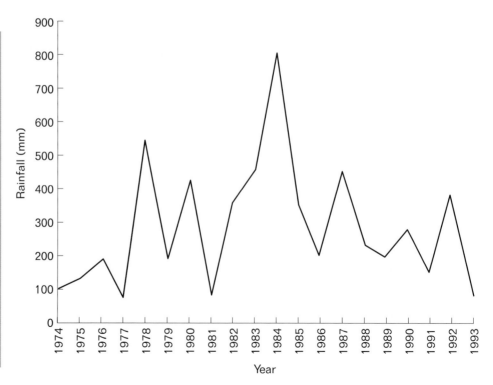

Questions ▶

1 The data below are rainfall (mm) records for the last twenty years from a site close to Oxford: 783, 509, 710, 577, 752, 634, 683, 655, 578, 608, 662, 704, 592, 571, 598, 473, 527, 796, 731, 699.
(**a**) Illustrate the data by means of (**i**) a line graph and (**ii**) a dispersion diagram.
(**b**) State the (**i**) maximum (**ii**) minimum (**iii**) range and (**iv**) inter-quartile range of the rainfall for the 20 year period.
(**c**) Which of these descriptive statistics is the best one in your opinion? Explain your answer.

▶ When the going gets tough …

Not every case is as easy! For example, there may be 21 or 22 figures, so that the number of observations is not divisible by 4. In those situations we have to make an informed guess at where the quartile would be.

If we take the case of 21 observations then the quartiles are at 5¼ and 15¾. In the following example (with rainfall for 1994 (210mm) added to the data in Figure 5.3) we can then make the estimate as follows.

Rainfall (mm)
75, 80, 84, 86, 125, 148, 184, 192, 195, 209, **210**, 235, 274, 361, 361, 390, 418, 452, 460, 538, 807.

The first quartile (5¼) lies a ¼ of the way between 125 and 148, while the third quartile (15¾) lies ¾ of the way between 361 and 390.

The first quartile is found by adding one quarter of the difference of 148 and 125 to 125, i.e.

$$125 + \frac{(148 - 125)}{4} = 130.75$$

The third quartile is found by adding ¾ of the difference of 390 and 361 from 361, i.e.

$$361 + \frac{3(390 - 361)}{4} = 382.75$$

Thus, the inter-quartile range is from 382·75 − 130·75, i.e. **252**.

In the next case there are 22 observations, as 1994 (210mm) and 1995 (175mm) has been added to the data from Figure 5.3.

Rainfall (mm)
75, 80, 84, 86, 125, 148, **175**, 184, 192, 195, 209, 210, 235, 274, 361, 361, 390, 418, 452, 460, 538, 807.

The quartiles now are found at 5½ and 16½ (as each quarter is 5½ in size). Thus the first quartile is found half-way between the 5th and 6th figures, 125 and 148 (i.e. 136·5), and the third quartile is found half-way between the 16th and 17th values, 361 and 390 (i.e. 375·5). Thus the inter-quartile range in this case is from 375·5 − 136·5, i.e. **239**.

In the final example there are now 23 observations. Rainfall for 1996 (400mm) has now been added.

Rainfall (mm)
75, 80, 84, 86, 125, 148, 175, 184, 192, 195, 209, 210, 235, 274, 361, 361, 390, **400**, 418, 452, 460, 538, 807.

The procedure is as before. Given that there are 23 observations, the quartiles are now located every 5¾ readings (i.e. 23 ÷ 4). Thus the first quartile is found ¾ of the way from the 5th value to the 6th, and the third quartile is found ¼ of the way from the 17th value to the 18th. Thus, the first quartile is: $125 + \frac{3(148 - 125)}{4} = 142.25$

The third quartile is:

$$390 + \frac{(400 - 390)}{4} = 392.5$$

Thus the inter-quartile range in this case is 392·5 − 142·25, i.e. **250·25**.

Spearman's rank correlation coefficient (Rs) is one of the most widely-used statistics in Geography. It is relatively quick and easy to do and only requires that data are available on the **ordinal** (ranked) scale, although interval or ratio data can be transformed into ranks very simply. It is called a 'rank' correlation because only the ranks are correlated and not the actual values. The use of Rs allows us to decide whether or not there is a **correlation** (relationship) between two sets of data. In some cases it is obvious whether a correlation exists or not (as shown in Figure 5.6). However, in most cases it is not so clear cut, and to avoid subjective comments we use Rs to bring in a certain amount of objectivity.

▶ Procedure

1 State the **null hypothesis (H$_0$)**, for example, there is no relationship between slope angle and soil depth. The **alternative hypothesis (H$_1$)** is that there *is* a relationship between slope angle and soil depth.

Fig. 5.6 Some Spearman's rank correlation coefficients (Rs)

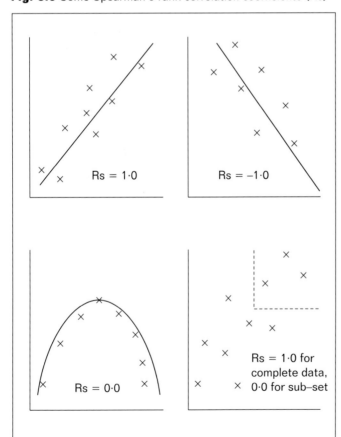

Rs = 1·0

Rs = −1·0

Rs = 0·0

Rs = 1·0 for complete data, 0·0 for sub–set

2 Rank both sets of data from highest to lowest (i.e. the highest value gets rank 1, the second highest 2, and so on). In the case of joint ranks, find the average rank, e.g. if two values occupy positions two and three they both take on rank 2·5, if three values occupy positions four, five and six, they all take rank 5.

3 Using the formula $Rs = 1 - \dfrac{6\,\Sigma d^2}{n^3 - n}$

work out the correlation, where '*d*' refers to the difference between ranks and '*n*' the number of observations.

4 Compare the computed Rs with the critical values in the statistical tables.

Worked example

Slope angle (cm)	Soil depth	Rank slope	Rank soil	Difference (d)	Difference^2 (d^2)
5·5	60	9	= 1·5	7·5	56·25
11·5	48	8	3	5	25
12	33	7	4	3	9
13	18	6	9	3	9
25	22	2	8	6	36
22	29	3	5	2	4
18	24	5	= 6·5	1·5	2·25
26	24	1	= 6·5	5·5	30·25
20	12	4	10	6	36
3	60	10	= 1·5	8·5	72·25
					$\Sigma d^2 = \mathbf{280}$

$$Rs = 1 - \frac{6\,\Sigma d^2}{n^3 - n} = 1 - \frac{6 \times 280}{10^3 - 10} = 1 - \frac{1\,680}{990} = 1 - 1\cdot697 = -0\cdot697$$

Now we have the computed value we compare it to the critical values. For a sample of 10, these values are 0·564 for 95% significance and 0·746 for 99% significance. In this example it is clear that the relationship is strong, i.e. there is more than 95% chance that there is a relationship between the data. The fact that the correlation is -0·966 shows that it is an **inverse relationship** (i.e. that as one variable increases the other decreases), thus as slope angle increases (or goes up) soil depth decreases. The next stage would be to offer explanations for the relationship.

If the computed value exceeds the critical values in Figure 5.6 we can say that we are 95% or 99% sure that there is a relationship between the sets of data. In other words, there is only a 5% or 1% chance that there is no relationship between the data.

Fig. 5.7 Levels of significance

N	Significance level 95%	Significance level 99%
4	1·00	–
5	0·90	1·00
6	0·83	0·94
7	0·71	0·89
8	0·64	0·83
9	0·60	0·78
10	0·56	0·75
12	0·51	0·71
14	0·46	0·65
16	0·43	0·60
18	0·40	0·56
20	0·38	0·53
22	0·36	0·51
24	0·34	0·49
26	0·33	0·47
28	0·32	0·45
30	0·31	0·42

▶ Limitations

It is important to realise that Spearman's rank has its weaknesses. It has a number of limitations which must be considered:

◆ it requires a sample size of at least seven

◆ it tests for linear relationships and would give an answer of '0' for data such as river discharge and frequency (see Figure 5.6) which follows a curvilinear pattern (with few very low or very high flows and a large number of medium flows)

◆ it is easy to make false correlations, e.g. between summer temperatures in the UK and infant mortality rates in India

◆ the question of scale is always important, e.g. a survey of river sediment rates and discharge for the whole of a drainage system may give a strong correlation, whereas analysis of just the upper catchments gives a much lower result.

As always, statistics are tools to be used. They are only part of the analysis, and we must be aware of their limits.

Questions ▶

Study the data below which shows settlement size and rates of crime.

1. State the null hypothesis.

2. Set out the data in a table as shown on page 54.

3. Rank both sets of data from high to low (highest = rank 1).

4. Work out the difference in ranks.

5. Find the square of the differences.

6. Add up the figures in the final column to find $\sum d^2$.

7. Using this figure work out the correlation between size of settlement and number of crimes:
$$Rs = 1 - \frac{6\sum d^2}{n^3 - n}$$

8. Compare your answer with the critical values in Figure 5.7. How significant is your result?

9. How do you explain the relationship between settlement size and amount of crime?

Settlement	Size	Rates of crime
Merton	339	4
Fencott & Murcott	203	5
Horton	441	34
Beckley	581	23
Noke	126	1
Elsfield	76	1
Woodeaton	104	4
Islip	601	25
Charlton	408	20
Oddington	89	1

NEAREST NEIGHBOUR INDEX (NNI)

Much of Geography is concerned with distributions in space. Some of the most important distributions that we have to consider include rural settlements and the distribution of functions in an urban area. The spatial distribution of settlements in an area can be described by looking at a map. This may lead us to conclude that the settlements are scattered, dispersed or concentrated. However, the main weakness with the visual method is that it is subjective (individuals differ in their interpretation of the pattern). Some objective measure is required and this is provided by the NNI.

There are three main types of pattern which can be distinguished: uniform or regular, clustered or aggregated, and random.

The points may represent settlements or indeed any feature which can be regarded as being located at a specific point, such as settlements, shops, factories, trees, etc. If the pattern is regular the distance between any one point and its nearest neighbour should be approximately the same as from any other point. If the pattern is clustered then many points will be found a short distance from each other and there will be large areas of the map without any points. A random distribution normally has a mixture of some clustering and some regularity.

The technique most commonly used to analyse these patterns is the **nearest neighbour index (NNI)**. It is a measure of the spatial distribution of points, and is derived from the average distance between each point and its nearest neighbour. This figure is then compared to computed values which state whether the pattern is:

◆ regular (NNI = 2·15)

◆ clustered (NNI = 0)

◆ random (NNI = 1·0).

Thus a value below 1·0 shows a tendency towards clustering, a value of above 1·0 a tendency towards uniformity.

The formula for the NNI looks somewhat daunting at first, but, like most statistics, is extremely straightforward providing care is taken.

$$NNI = 2\bar{D} \sqrt{(N \div A)}$$

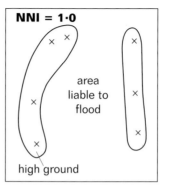
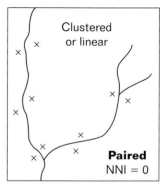
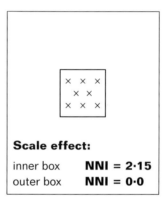
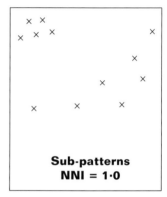

Fig. 5.8 Patterns and their nearest neighbour index (NNI)

$\bar{D}$ is the average distance between each point and its nearest neighbour, and is calculated by finding $\Sigma d \div N$ (d refers to each individual distance); N the number of points under study and A the size of the area under study. It is important that you use the same units for distance and area (e.g. metres or km but not a mixture).

Worked example

For example, a survey of the nine villages of Otmoor (see Figure 6.23 page 79) produced the following results:

Village	Nearest neighbour	Distance (km)
Merton	Fencott	1·5
Islip	Noke	2·0
Noke	Islip	2·0
Beckley	Horton	3·0
Horton	Beckley	3·0
Fencott	Murcott	1·0
Murcott	Fencott	1·0
Charlton	Oddington	1·5
Oddington	Charlton	1·5
Woodeaton	Elsfield	2·0
Elsfield	Woodeaton	2·0
		Σd 20·5

Formula

$$NNI = 2\bar{D}\sqrt{\left(\frac{N}{A}\right)}$$

$$\bar{D} = \frac{\Sigma d}{N} = \frac{20\cdot5}{11} = 1\cdot9$$

$$NNI = 2 \times 1\cdot9 \times \sqrt{\left(\frac{11}{64}\right)}$$

$$NNI = \mathbf{1\cdot57}$$

The results of NNI vary anywhere between 0 and 2·15. There is a continuum of values and any distribution lies somewhere between the two extremes. The answer in our worked example suggests a significant degree of clustering.

There are important points to bear in mind when using the nearest neighbour index.

◆ Where do you measure from – the centre or the edge of a settlement? Some discretion is needed.

◆ Do you measure with a straight line or by road (or water)?

◆ What is the definition of whatever is being studied? For example, do you include *all* settlements *and* individual houses, or just those settlements above a certain size?

◆ Why do we take the nearest neighbour? Why not the third or fourth nearest?

◆ What is the effect of paired distributions (see Figure 5.8)?

◆ One overall index may obliterate important sub-patterns (see Figure 5.8).

◆ The choice of the area and the size of the area studied, can completely alter the result and make a clustered pattern appear regular and vice-versa (see Figure 5.8).

◆ Although the NNI may suggest a random pattern, it may be that the controlling factor (e.g. soil type or altitude) is itself randomly distributed, and that the settlements are in fact located in anything but a random fashion.

Questions ▶

The maps below show the distribution of banks and post boxes in part of a city centre.

1 Label both sets of points **A** to **G**.

2 Measure the distance from each point to its nearest neighbour.

3 Set out your answer as on page 56.

4 Add up the values of *d* and divide by N (7 in this case) to find $\bar{D}$.

5 Put this value into the formula $NNI = 2\bar{D}\sqrt{(N \div A)}$. (**NB** N = 7, A = 1km^2 or 1,000,000m^2)

6 What does the answer tell you about the distribution of banks and the distribution of post boxes? Explain the reasons why they vary.

Fig. 5.9 Distribution of banks and post boxes

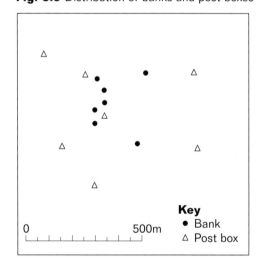

Key
● Bank
△ Post box

Fig. 5.10 The statistical significance of NNI values

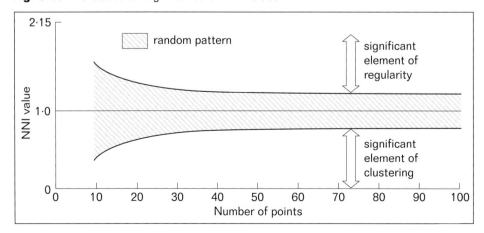

COMPLETING A PERSONAL

All projects need to be carefully planned in terms of time as well as content. To help you plan properly, complete Figure 6.1 with your own dates so that you know when all the deadlines are. Similarly you should fill in a form like the Project Planning Sheet on page 62 to make clear the plan for your project.

Fig. 6.1 Deadlines

		DEADLINE DATE
	Proposal: outline of project	
A	Introduction (background essay on topic)	
	Pilot study (to see if the project will work)	
B	Data collection (methods)	
C	Presentation of data	
D	Data interpretation	
E	Understanding and explanation of data	
F	Evaluation	
	Bibliography	

Each of the items A–F in Figure 6.1 can be broken down into sections.

▶ A Introduction to the enquiry

There are at least four parts to the Introduction:

◆ the geographical theme and background (e.g. shopping centres, central places, traffic and accessibility)

◆ the geographical location (its relative site and situation)

◆ the specific hypotheses (or ideas) that you are going to test

◆ a brief description of the data you will collect and how you will test and present it.

All four parts need to be described, and the location should be shown by a freehand map. The key is to explain and justify the title, methods and techniques that you will use.

1 Geographical background This refers to the geographical theories or models that are used to try to explain your enquiry, such as the use of

central place theory to explain settlement patterns, or the factors that explain agricultural and industrial land use models. Similarly, in physical projects you may discuss the factors influencing certain features or processes. Examiners' reports have shown that this section is often not very well done; you should refer to articles and relevant literature here.

2 Geographical location This is important. It is the geographical setting. The best enquiries state why the area under study is good for that particular project. Make sure that you include the area's site as well as its regional situation. For physical studies, describe and comment upon the physical background, e.g. geology, structure, landforms, and soil/vegetation characteristics.

3 Hypotheses These are the ideas that you intend to test. They arise from a combination of the theories (models) and the area. There may be a number of sub-hypotheses that explore different aspects of the idea, e.g. the influence of age, rock type and aspect on the rate of weathering on a gravestone. For each hypothesis or idea that you investigate you should describe what you expect to find, and explain why.

4 Data Having covered these three aspects you should state briefly what data you will collect, how you will analyse it, and how you intend to present it. This is an introduction to the second section, Data collection, and is a useful way of rounding off the Introduction.

Having stated the hypotheses to be tested, it is important to follow this up with clear points describing:

◆ what type of data you need to examine your hypotheses

◆ from which sources you intend to collect your data; state which primary sources (fieldwork methods) and which secondary sources (printed matter) you will use

◆ what type of sampling procedure (e.g. random, systematic, stratified, transect) you intend to use for each type of data, and why

◆ what methods of fieldwork and equipment you will use to collect each set of data, and why you will use them

INVESTIGATIVE ENQUIRY

◆ the methods of statistical analysis that you intend to use, and why.

You should use a copy of the Project Planning Sheet on page 62 to help you structure your data collection.

Pilot Study

A pilot study is a trial study to see if it is possible to carry out your project. For example, if you are investigating the characteristics of a river, you need to find out whether you can gain access to the river. Similarly, if you are carrying out a shopping survey, you need to get permission from the local shop owners before you do your survey. For questionnaires, it is worth trialling a mini-questionnaire to see how it works; there may be questions people refuse to answer or which elicit long rambling answers it is hard to quantify. The questionnaire can then be modified to take problems like this into account.

▶ B Data collection methods

Use as many different techniques as possible to gather information, e.g. interviews, observations, surveys, questionnaires, maps and looking at figures. Describe and justify each method. Some of these are primary (your own fieldwork) and some are secondary (published statistics, maps, diagrams, etc.) You need both. Describe the use of primary fieldwork methods and in particular the method or equipment used to collect each type of information. Equally, describe and explain the use of secondary sources, e.g. the census, parish records.

Explain clearly how you decided to use your figures, maps, answers to questions, etc. Some reasoning is necessary here – that is, justify why you used that method or source. Explain in detail, for example, how you questioned people, collected census figures, obtained maps, etc. Write this up almost like the method for a scientific experiment. You can use a planning sheet here stating when you collected data, where from, at what time, places you visited, observations you made, interviews you conducted, etc. If you are using a questionnaire then you must justify the questions that you use, e.g. why have you recorded age and sex of respondents in a shopping survey? You need a range of methods to obtain full marks.

▶ C Presentation of data

Data presentation, data interpretation and the understanding of ideas and explanations are best combined rather than treated separately. This is because it is best if under each graph, map or chart you describe the results (pattern, trend and/or association) and then try to explain them (using material that you covered in the Introduction concerning the theme of your project). However, to keep these instructions relatively simple, the three sections are treated separately here.

Examiners' reports say that too many candidates fail to use a range of presentation techniques and that they use inappropriate ones. Try to integrate the techniques and analytical commentary (Fig. 6.2) to gain the maximum mark possible. If you don't, you may find that the examiner skips the section where you use ten or more pie charts and bar graphs, because without any description or explanation these are exceedingly dull.

There are a variety of different techniques for presenting your data.

◆ Maps: locational maps, flow-line maps, isoline maps, dot maps, proportional symbol maps, choropleth maps, symbol maps, density and distribution maps, etc.

◆ Graphs: line graphs and scattergraphs for visual correlations; bar charts and histograms to show the frequency of data distribution; orientation graphs to show direction and frequency; cumulative frequency graphs.

◆ Tables: data set out in tabular form – grouped, categorised, ranked or just listed.

◆ Photos, diagrams (pie charts, cross-sections) and field sketches should be used throughout the study to illustrate and explain each stage. Annotate them and use them to describe or explain geographical ideas.

◆ Statistical methods: probably the most important set of methods describing your data or showing quantitative relationships.

◆ Descriptive statistics: methods of describing the central tendency of data, e.g. mode, median and mean. Other methods such as percentages and ratios should also be used.

Methods for relating or associating data could also be used (computer programs are excellent for processing such data), e.g. rank correlation techniques.

Remember to discuss the significance of your results by using the appropriate tests. Also, justify each method used and describe the problems encountered in using such techniques.

For top marks, use a wide range of maps, sketches, statistical diagrams, photographs, tables of figures, graphs, bar charts, pie charts, scattergraphs, drawings, etc. to display your data. Photographs or

Fig. 6.2 Presentation techniques in your project

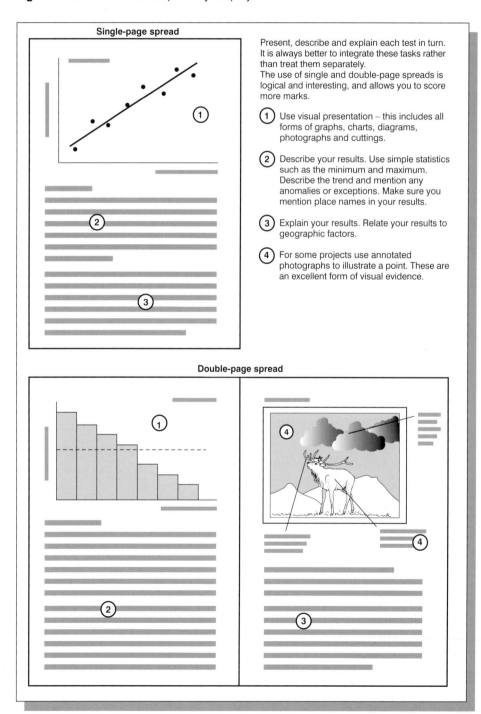

Single-page spread

Present, describe and explain each test in turn. It is always better to integrate these tasks rather than treat them separately.
The use of single and double-page spreads is logical and interesting, and allows you to score more marks.

(1) Use visual presentation – this includes all forms of graphs, charts, diagrams, photographs and cuttings.

(2) Describe your results. Use simple statistics such as the minimum and maximum. Describe the trend and mention any anomalies or exceptions. Make sure you mention place names in your results.

(3) Explain your results. Relate your results to geographic factors.

(4) For some projects use annotated photographs to illustrate a point. These are an excellent form of visual evidence.

Double-page spread

newspaper cuttings should be labelled to show the examiner how you have made use of them, and that you have not just stuck them in to make the project bigger or prettier. Do not simply use them as 'extras', but integrate the diagrams, maps, newspaper articles etc. into the text by giving each illustration a reference number (e.g. 'Table 1'), and then refer to it (e.g. 'see Table 1') in your written work.

Examples of data sheets, questionnaires, equations, etc. that you used should be included. If you have done a questionnaire, you do not need to put all the completed ones in the appendix; one example will do. However, you do need to hand in the others with your project so that if the examiner calls for your project the questionnaires can be submitted.

▶ D Interpretation of data

◆ After each graph or technique, describe fully the results or trend or association (using simple descriptive statistics). What do your results tell you? Describe your findings in detail by quoting the evidence from your methods of analysis.

◆ Describe the pattern on your graph. What does the graph show?

◆ Do the graphs/diagrams etc. help to answer the question set? How?

◆ Make comments to link the data. For example, show how one diagram, graph or map relates to others.

◆ Draw conclusions from the data.

▶ E Understanding and explanation of data

◆ Now briefly explain the relationship or pattern that you have found. Compare the results of the data analysis against standard models and theories.

◆ Link what you have found out in your enquiry to what you have studied in the syllabus. For example, if you looked at shopping, have you talked about high-order and low-order shops, shopping hierarchies, etc.? If your investigation is on leisure, have you linked this to the amount of leisure time people have, spheres of influence of leisure centres, how accessible places are, etc.? These things should be mentioned in your

Introduction (the geographical theme) and need to be discussed now in relation to your findings.

◆ Having described your results, now explain and discuss them. Why have you arrived at such results? Do they confirm or refute your hypotheses?

▶ F Evaluation

Your project is likely to be slightly less than perfect, and you need to show the examiner that you are aware of this. It is important to realise that you will not be marked down for showing an awareness of the limitations of methods, results and conclusions. Indeed, you are more likely to be penalised if you do not include a brief section like this. There may be limits to where and when you could carry out a survey, or the number of people that you could interview; constraints of expense; measurements of rivers may be hampered by floods or droughts; and so on.

What you need to do is to make an assessment and state whether or not these limitations have impaired your project. If they have, then your results are likely to be compromised, and so will any conclusions that you draw. For example, a survey of tourists to Oxford on a Tuesday afternoon in April found that most people were attracted to the university buildings and the colleges, and listed the poor weather as their main criticism. Had the survey taken place in another kind of tourist destination, the attractions listed would have been very different. Similarly, had the survey taken place in July or August the weather might not have been mentioned as a problem; on the other hand, congestion due to too many tourists might have been mentioned. This example shows that the methods (including the date and time of any survey) produce results that can affect our conclusions and, therefore, our evaluation. Another survey at another time would give a different set of results and conclusions.

▶ Bibliography

At the end of the project you should make a list of any books, articles or other sources of information that you have used for your project. You do not need to include notes that you have made in class, only the extra material you used.

Fig. 6.3 Project planning sheet

PROJECT PLANNING SHEET										
NAME				**TEACHER**			**TITLE OF PROJECT**			
Hypotheses (ideas to test)	Primary (own) data	Secondary (published) data	Graphic and cartographic (map) techniques (e.g. flow lines, choropleth maps, bar charts)	Statistical techniques, (e.g. percentages, means, Spearman's Rank)	Links with geographical theory, factors or models					
Evaluation of:	Methods		Techniques		Results/conclusions					

SAMPLING

In most investigations it is not possible to survey everything in the study area. For example, you cannot ask every shopper on a busy Saturday what they are buying; similarly, in a study of sand dune vegetation it is not possible to survey every plant in the whole area. As a result some form of selection is needed – this is called **sampling**.

The sample should be representative of your study area. For example, in a shopping survey, results would be affected if all questionnaires were asked to the customers of just one shop; and in a sand dune study it would be unwise just to sample the first 10 metres of beach.

▶ Methods of sampling

There are three principal methods of sampling, as follows.

Random sampling is where each member of a population has an equal chance of being selected. To select from this population, each member is assigned a number using computer-generated random number tables.

20	**17**	42	28	23	17	59	66	38	61	74
49	04	49	03	04	10	33	53	70	94	70
49	31	38	67	23	42	26	65	22	15	78
15	69	84	32	52	32	54	93	29	12	12
27	30	30	55	91	87					

For example, if we wanted to sample sand dune vegetation randomly, we might start from a central position in the dune complex. Using a table of random numbers we would select two numbers: the first number in the pair might represent distance and the second number compass direction. For instance, we might select the numbers '20' and '17': '20' would represent 20 metres, '17' would represent the compass direction. Obviously the numbers only go from '0' to '99', so we need to convert '17' to degrees, i.e. $360° ÷ 100 = 3·6°$.

Therefore, the number representing compass direction must be multiplied by $3·6°$ to convert to degrees. In this case, 17 x 3·6 = 61°.

So, the sample would be taken 20m away from the centre point at a bearing of 61° (see Figure 6.2).

Fig. 6.2 Random sampling

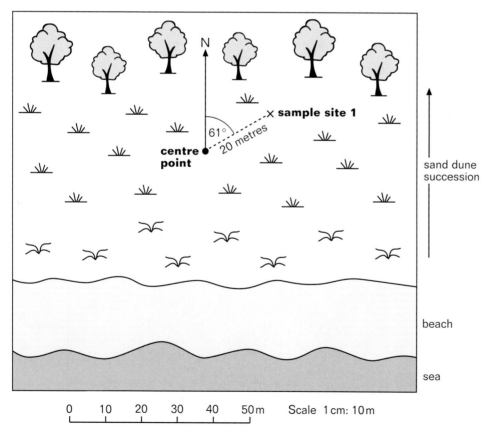

Systematic sampling is where each sample is selected in a regular manner. For example, this would mean taking a vegetation sample every 10 metres, or taking a sample at a series of points located at the intersection of a 10m grid (see Figure 6.3). This method avoids bunching and is simple and easy to apply.

Stratified sampling takes into account the relative proportion of different groups within the sample.

For example, in the sand dune investigation, two-thirds of the area may be managed and the rest unmanaged. Stratified sampling will select a representative sample from these two areas. If nine transects are to be selected, then the correct balance is six managed and three unmanaged. A random sampling design can be followed to select the transects in each group.

▶ Sample size

Many investigations fail because the size of the sample is too small – without a sufficient variety and number within the sample, results can be unrepresentative. Sample size should be greater than 30: this is much easier when asking 30 questionnaires than conducting 30 transects along a sand dune, e.g. in the sand dune investigation it is more realistic to take 30 readings along a single transect.

Fig. 6.3 Systematic sampling

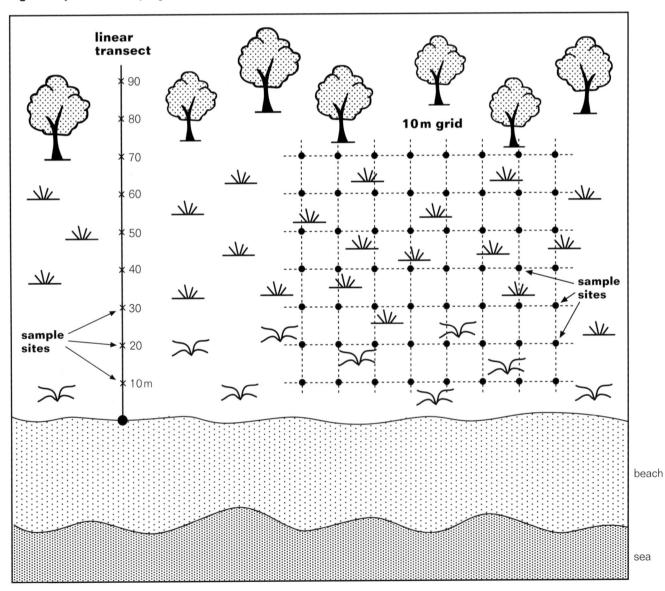

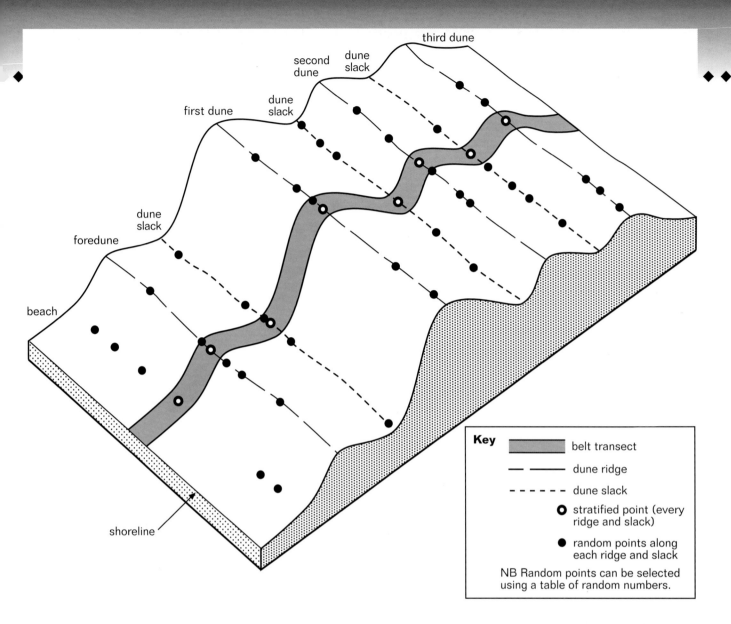

Fig. 6.4 Sampling in practice: stratified and random approaches combined

▶ Errors of data collection

◆ **Measurement error**: measuring the number of plant species (or even transect distance) is subject to a whole series of measurement errors.

◆ **Operator error**: one person will not measure the number or type of plant species in the same way as another – this is called bias. It can be estimated by setting up a controlled measurement of a small sub-sample.

◆ **Sampling error**: local differences mean that one sample will yield slightly different results than another.

QUESTIONNAIRES

Most investigations will use some form of **questionnaire** to collect primary data. A questionnaire survey can generate descriptive and explanatory data in the following forms:

◆ **background information** about your sample population (e.g. age, sex, occupation)

◆ **behavioural information** about what people do (e.g. how often they shop for a particular good)

◆ **attitudinal information** relating to what people think about a particular issue.

▶ Constructing a questionnaire

A successful questionnaire must be carefully planned. You must know how each question relates to the aims of your enquiry. Other considerations include the type of question to be asked, the layout and length of the questionnaire and the number and type of people to be asked.

▶ Type of question

A number of different types of question can be included in your questionnaire as follows.

◆ **Open questions** allow a space for the respondent to answer freely and give greater choice, but often result in data which is difficult to collate and group.

◆ **Closed questions** give a choice of responses and so limit the freedom of respondents. They are quicker and mean the data are already processed into different groups. Closed questions can take a number of different forms:
– yes/no choice
– multiple choice
– bi-polar semantic scales (where respondents are asked to rate something subjectively).

▶ Layout and length

The length of your questionnaire will depend on your aims. Certainly, you should try to keep your questions to a single page. The number of questions is also important: 7 to 10 questions is an appropriate number for a general survey.

The layout is equally important. Begin your questionnaire with background information and

then lead into the more specific and complex questions.

Remember to be sensitive and polite. Some people may be reluctant to give information on age, occupation or status.

▶ Pilot surveys

It is vital that you 'road test' your questionnaire before undertaking your full survey. Try your questions out on 10 people. This will highlight any questions which are difficult, poorly-worded or confusing. The questionnaire can then be amended.

Questions ▶

1 Questionnaires can be posted or conducted by a face-to-face interview. Which method is most likely to have:
(**a**) the highest response rate?
(**b**) the most chance of bias (i.e. asking a similar type of person rather than a more representative sample)?
(**c**) the ability to ask supplementary questions and clarify misunderstandings?

2 Figure 6.5 gives a questionnaire which could be used for a project on residential quality (see page 68). Figure 6.6 gives a similar questionnaire for a project on gentrification.
(**a**) Figure 6.5 asks respondents to rate the area from 1 to 5 (a bipolar semantic scale). What are the advantages and disadvantages of this type of question?
(**b**) Which of the questionnaires has the most open responses?
(**c**) What are the advantages of open responses?

Street _____   **Position** _____

important when displaying results on maps afterwards

Sex

☐ male   ☐ female

Age

☐ under 25   ☐ 26–40   ☐ 41–60   ☐ over 60

information which is basic but may explain people's differing attitudes to their area

What sort of housing do you live in?

☐ council housing
☐ privately rented (unfurnished)
☐ owned house
☐ privately rented (furnished)
☐ owned flat
☐ other (please specify) _____

will indicate the transience of the population which will affect housing quality

How long have you been living here?

☐ under 6 months   ☐ 6–12 months   ☐ 1–2 years
☐ 3–5 years   ☐ over 5 years   ☐ don't know

How much longer do you expect to live here?

☐ under 6 months   ☐ 6–12 months   ☐ 1–2 years
☐ 3–5 years   ☐ over 5 years   ☐ don't know

How would you rate this area on a scale of 1 to 5 in relation to: (1 = bad   5 = excellent   X = do not know)

noise	....	green areas	....	healthcare	....
pollution	....	shops	....	services for retired	....
heavy traffic	....	transport	....	libraries	....
crime	....	recreation	....	entertainment	....
housing quality	....	schools	....		

externalities that will affect housing quality

On a scale of 1 to 5 please give your views on the attraction of the following areas: (1 = not very desirable   5 = very desirable   X = do not know)

Hammersmith flyover	....	West Kensington	....	Shepherd's Bush	....
Brook Green	....	Brackenbury Village	....	Fulham (riverside)	....
Olympia	....	Goldhawk Road	....	Fulham (Queen's Club)	....

to find out different opinions of areas which may help to explain housing quality

Is the accommodation you have one that you occupy:

☐ alone   ☐ with partner/spouse   ☐ with family with children
☐ with friends   ☐ other   ☐ no response

will affect the transience of population of an area (family life-cycle model) and therefore the housing quality of the area

Fig. 6.5 Example of questionnaire on residential quality

1 How long have you lived in this area?
☐ 0-2 years   ☐ 3-5 years   ☐ 6-10 years   ☐ 11+ years

2 Where did you live prior to that?   town _____   borough _____

3 Is this your house: ☐ privately rented   ☐ owner occupied   ☐ council rented

4 What renovations have you made?   ☐ loft extension   ☐ conservatory   ☐ redecorating
others (please specify) _____

5 How many people live in your house? ....   6 How many bedrooms? ....

7 What is your marital status?   ☐ single   ☐ married   ☐ divorced

8 With regard to work, do you consider yourself:
☐ retired   ☐ part-time   ☐ full-time   ☐ unemployed

9 If part-time or full-time, what is your occupation and rank? _____

10 Do you have a car? ☐ yes   ☐ no   Do you have a second car? ☐ yes   ☐ no

year _____   make _____   year _____   make _____

11 Where do you work? _____

12 Mode of travel?   ☐ car   ☐ bus   ☐ tube   ☐ bike   ☐ walk

13 Do you have any children?   ☐ yes   ☐ no

14 If yes, how many? ....   how old? ....

15 What school(s) do they go to? _____

16 Why did you choose to live here?   prices
proximity to: communications
workplace
services
good restaurants
other _____

1 ☐☐☐☐☐ 5
☐☐☐☐☐
☐☐☐☐☐
☐☐☐☐☐
☐☐☐☐☐

17 Why did you choose to live in this street? _____

Fig. 6.6 Example of questionnaire on gentrification

Does the thought of living in a small town or village appeal to you? For many families it represents security, friendliness and a pleasant place to live. But for others it is a source of hardship. A recent report shows just how much rural services have declined in recent decades. So what are rural villages really like to live in and what is it like to live in a rural area?

The Rural Development Commission's 1991 survey of rural services revealed that:

◆ 39% of parishes had no shop

◆ 40% had no post office (see Photo 6.1)

◆ 51% had no school

◆ 29% had no village hall

◆ 73% had no daily bus service

◆ fewer than 10% had a bank or building society, a nursery or day-care centre, a dentist or a daily train service.

Where they existed, services tended to be concentrated in larger villages and market towns. Overall, the services which most people take for granted are few and far between in the countryside. With the lack of public transport rural people are heavily reliant on cars to reach essential services, recreational or other facilities. Population changes have led to most rural areas having above average numbers of elderly people and below average numbers of 16–20 year olds.

(*Source: Rural Development Commission, 1994*)

▶ Hypotheses

The hypotheses that we are testing here are that:

◆ the larger the settlement (in population size) the greater the amount and range of services that it contains

◆ the greater the distance from Oxford the larger the settlement and the more services there are

◆ the settlement pattern on Otmoor is regular, as predicted by **central place theory**

◆ rates of crime are higher in larger settlements than in smaller ones.

Photo 6.1 The Old Post Office, Islip. What are the implications for people without a car?

▶ Data collection methods

There are a number of ways of collecting the data. It is best to collect as many types as possible, so that a full examination and critique can be made.

◆ **Observations**: in each village record the number of houses, the number of services and list all the services that are found there (e.g. three schools, one post-box, a pub, etc.). Also carry out a survey into the age and likely origins of the village. For this you will have to look at the age of buildings (some should have dates on them, especially churches and gravestones), the characteristics of the site (close to a river, woodland, high ground, south facing, confluence of streams, etc.).

◆ **Census data**: this will provide data on the population size of each village or parish (check carefully). Other population figures may be available from the County Council.

◆ **Ordnance Survey maps**: these provide a great deal of information on the physical size of each village, its accessibility (road and rail), distance from nearby large urban centres and information on selected services (e.g. schools, churches, post offices, public houses). It would be possible to derive a hierarchy from an investigation of OS maps on their own. The maps can also be used to work out a nearest neighbour index for the Otmoor villages (see page 56). According to the NNI, a perfectly regular central place network will have a value of 2·15.

◆ **Questionnaires**: a simple questionnaire to discover patterns of shopping for high- and low-order goods in the area could show the importance (or sphere of influence) of each village.

◆ **Bus timetables**: these show which villages are most accessible in terms of the number of buses per day and their destination.

◆ **Crime records**: these are available from Regional Offices (e.g. Thames Valley Police in Kidlington) and provide information on the type and number of crimes in villages and districts.

Fig. 6.20 Settlements and number of services

Settlement	Size	No. of services
Merton	339	8
Fencott & Murcott	203	14
Horton	441	14
Beckley	581	16
Noke	126	9
Elsfield	76	4
Woodeaton	104	5
Islip	601	17
Charlton	408	14
Oddington	89	7

Fig. 6.21 Testing for a correlation (see page 54)

Spearman's rank correlation coefficient uses the formula:
$$Rs = 1 - \frac{6\Sigma d^2}{n^3 - n}$$
where d is the difference in ranks and n is the number of observations.

Settlement	Rank size	Rank services	Difference (d)	d^2
Merton	5	7	2	4
Fencott & Murcott	6	4	2	4
Horton	3	4	1	1
Beckley	2	2	0	0
Noke	7	6	1	1
Elsfield	10	10	0	0
Woodeaton	8	9	1	1
Islip	1	1	0	0
Charlton	4	4	0	0
Oddington	9	8	1	1
				$\Sigma d^2 = \mathbf{12}$

$$Rs = 1 - \frac{6 \times 12}{10^3 - 10}$$

$$= 1 - \frac{72}{990} = 1 - 0.072 = \mathbf{0.928}$$

▶ Techniques

For the hypothesis 'the larger the settlement the greater the amount and range of services', these techniques could be used:

◆ **simple descriptive statistics**, e.g. maximum, minimum, range (see page 50)

◆ **scattergraph** of population size and number of services (see page 37)

◆ **Spearman's rank correlation** (see page 54) between population size and number of services

◆ **proportional pie chart** (see page 38) for number and type of services (high/low-order goods).

Fig. 6.22 Scattergraph to show the relationship between population size and number of services

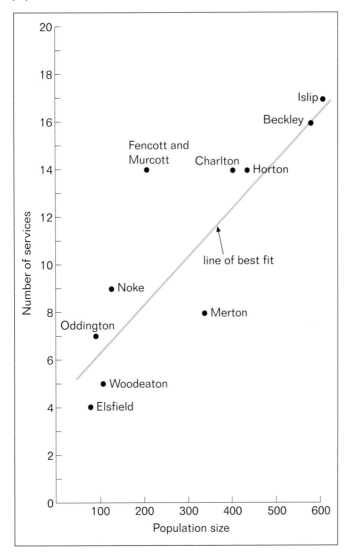

For the hypothesis 'the greater the distance from Oxford the greater the amount and range of services', the techniques mentioned above could also be used. In addition a **flow diagram** (see page 42) to show bus routes to Oxford could be drawn.

For the hypothesis 'the settlement pattern is regular and corresponds to the model central place distribution', these techniques could be used:

◆ **proportional circles** to show location and size of settlements (see page 38)

◆ **nearest neighbour index** (see page 56).

For the hypothesis 'rates of crime are higher in larger settlements than in smaller ones', these techniques could be used:

◆ **scattergraphs**

◆ **proportional pie charts**

◆ **Spearman's rank correlation**.

▶ Presentation

The scattergraph in Figure 6.22 shows that as population size increases the number of services increases. The largest village is Islip with a population of 601 and 17 services, while Elsfield has just 76 inhabitants and only four services. There a couple of anomalies to this pattern. For example, Fencott and Murcott have only 203 people and 14 services while Merton has 339 people and 8 services. The Spearman's rank correlation of 0·93 (which is 99% significant) shows that there is a strong association between village size and number of services. This is largely explained through the need for a large threshold population to support certain high-order goods, which are therefore located in larger villages.

The proportional circles (see Figure 6.23) show the pattern of settlement distribution in Otmoor. The central area is largely free of settlements and the villages are spread regularly around the moor on elevated ground. The nearest neighbour index of 1·57 indicates a pattern that is significantly regular in pattern as well as in site (i.e. the villages are regularly found on high ground).

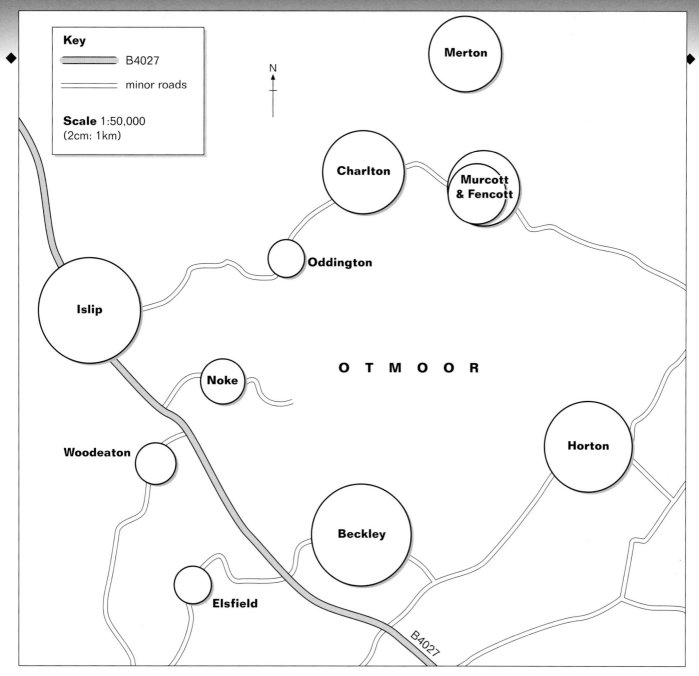

Fig. 6.23 The village of Otmoor and its surrounding area

▶ Limitations of this project

◆ Do all services receive the same value (e.g. is a church more or less important than a public house)?

◆ What constitutes a service (e.g. a bus stop, a letter box, a mobile library)?

◆ Where do you measure the boundary of the village from (e.g. from the village name post, the first house)?

◆ How do you record services that are found between villages (e.g. a farm shop, a teashop, a garage)?

▶ Strengths of this project

◆ A wide variety of data are available and easily collected.

◆ A large number of techniques and skills can be used.

◆ There are conflicting views (values and attitudes) over the benefits of living in a small village.

◆ The data are accurate and reliable – if recorded properly and carefully.

◆ The enquiry is local in scale.

◆ A small area yields excellent results.

LOCATION OF URBAN FUNCTIONS

Have you ever wondered why there are so many banks and estate agents in the centre of a town, but there are often few schools, if any? And why there are so many hypermarkets, garden centres and garages on the edge of a town, but very few solicitors or banks?

▶ Hypotheses

The main hypothesis that we are testing is that urban functions vary in their locational preference.

We can also test a number of sub-hypotheses, as follows.

◆ Financial services (e.g. banks and solicitors) are located close to the central business district because this is the most accessible area of a town or city.

◆ DIY and garden centres tend to be located on the outskirts of town where more land is available for large retail outlets and car parks. These stores are very accessible for people with cars.

◆ Primary schools are scattered around the urban area so that they are close to residential areas.

▶ Data collection methods

There are a number of ways in which the data can be collected as follows.

◆ **Observation**: the most obvious way is to observe the town by walking around and recording the exact location of each outlet on your map, although this can be rather time consuming. When recording the services on a map, use a different colour for each service and also record the name of each facility. This is essential for later descriptions of the distribution you have found. The easiest and most efficient way of completing this is to decide beforehand on the order in which you will visit the roads. NB All roads should be visited.

◆ **Secondary data**: you could use *Thompson's Local Directory* to find out where facilities and services are located. This is also a useful first step, as it gives you a rough idea of how many there are and where each one is. However, *Thompson's Local Directory* only takes into account advertisers, and unless you know the numbering of the streets it does not show you the exact location of each outlet.

Photo 6.2 Clustering of banks and building societies in central Witney

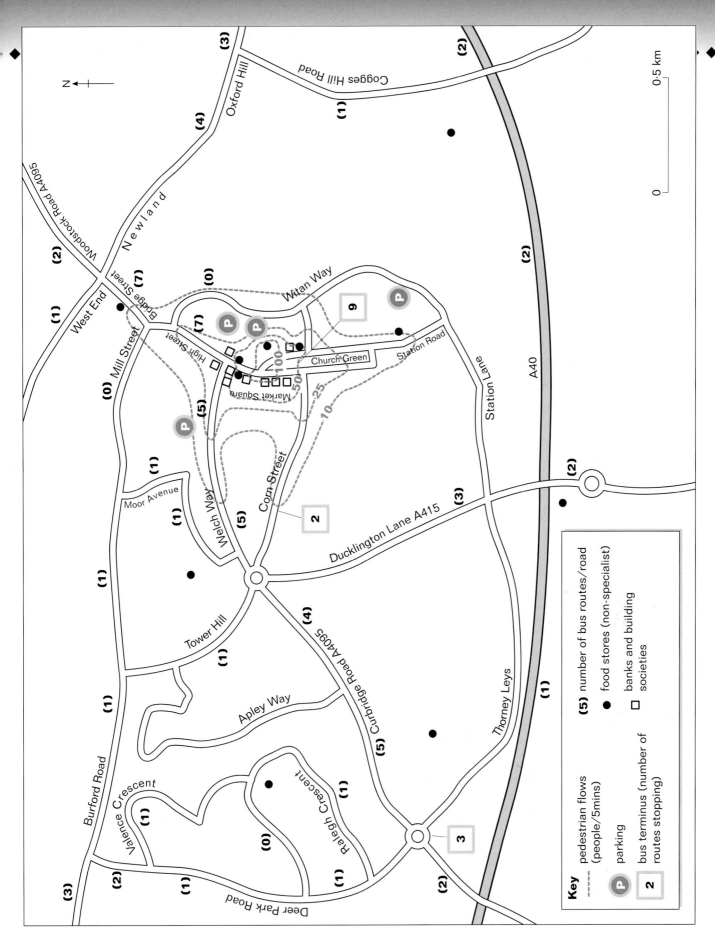

Fig. 6.24 Accessibility to banks, building societies and food stores in Witney

- **Information centres**: these are often located in public libraries or council offices, and they may be able to supply you with the information required (however, the same constraints as for *Thompson's Local Directory* need to be considered.

- **Ordnance Survey maps**: these will help you to decide upon accessibility. The maps show the pattern of roads, rail networks, car parks, etc. which you can use to work out which areas are accessible, and for whom.

- **Pedestrian flow**: a series of surveys are needed to work out the areas which are most accessible to pedestrians (this is because banks, solicitors and high street shops tend to be found in areas which are accessible to pedestrians rather than motorists).

- **Estate agents' maps**: these road maps are very useful for small- and medium-sized towns, and are usually available free (or with a small charge). You can record the location of each facility on those maps. Be careful about the scale of the map as a little mathematics may be needed to convert miles into kilometres (five miles is approximately eight kilometres).

- **Car parking spaces**: these can be found by observation, or alternatively by contacting the local council transport department who can provide information on public car parks (other private car parks will have to be surveyed).

A problem that will become apparent when carrying out your data collection is that of definitions. For example, do you include building societies as banks, and grocers as supermarkets, and do you differentiate between garages that sell petrol and those that do not? You will have to decide on your definitions, the decision is yours, but you must justify them.

Sets of five contrasting services could include:

- banks, post offices, florists, newsagents, primary schools

- solicitors, launderettes, garages, secondary schools, antique shops

- building societies, supermarkets, chemists, fast-food places, car parks

- dentists, DIY stores, clothes shops, hotels, public phones

- doctor's surgery, toy shops, recreation grounds, churches, pubs

- book shops, bookmakers (betting shops), off-licences, hotels, WCs

- butchers, bike shops, electrical shops, hairdressers, shoe shops

- furniture stores, bakers, estate agents, sports centres, nightclubs.

It is best to compare contrasting services or functions which have very different locational requirements. For example, banks, solicitors and restaurants tend to be found in highly-central accessible areas (why?), but DIY stores, garages and garden centres are increasingly found at the margins of towns (why?). However, schools and post offices tend to be distributed throughout the whole of the built up area. Why is this so?

▶ Techniques

- A **dot map** showing the distribution of each service. **Annotated photographs** (see page 48) to show clustering of services and **simple statistics** to describe the characteristics of the functions found in the town (see page 50).

- The **nearest neighbour index** (see page 56) to show the degree of clustering, regularity or randomness of the distribution in question.

- **Isolines** to show pedestrian flows (see page 43).

- **Flow lines** to show bus routes and levels of accessibility (see page 42).

- **Pictograms** to show how car parking varies between central locations and out-of-town positions (see page 41).

▶ Presentation

First, show the location of each service on a separate map. Describe the distribution: refer to the number of facilities that there are and where they are (name places). Mention areas where you were surprised that a facility was not found. For example, the distribution of banks and building societies in Witney is highly concentrated along

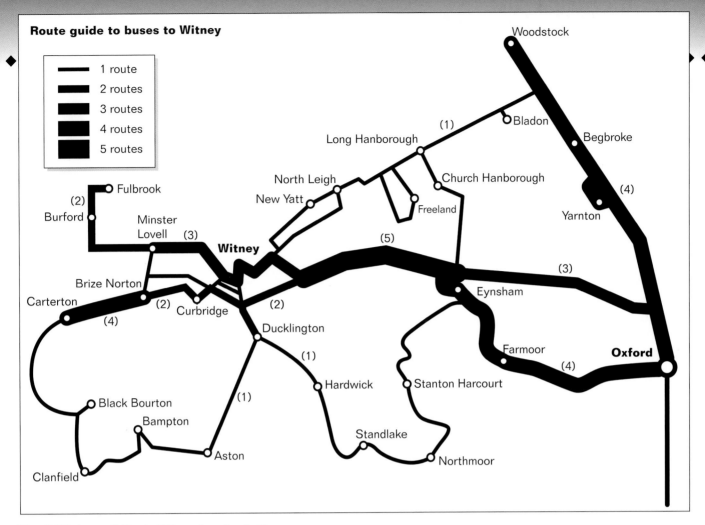

Fig. 6.25 Accessibility to Witney from local villages

High Street and Market Square. No fewer than nine outlets are found very close to each other. On the other hand, food stores are spread throughout the town centre and the residential areas.

Next, work out the nearest neighbour index for each distribution. For banks and building societies in Witney, the answer is approximately 0·12, indicating a very significant degree of clustering. Explain this distribution in relation to accessibility, public and private transport, parking facilities, demand and population distribution. An isoline map showing pedestrian flows highlights areas which are most accessible, and a flow diagram of bus routes shows that the most accessible part of the town is the Market Square.

▶ Limitations of this project

◆ **Definitions**: how do you distinguish between garages that sell petrol and those that do not? Should hypermarkets, grocers and garages that sell food be treated the same? What if a service

is only open for a small part of the time, for example, a sub-post-office?

◆ The **nearest neighbour index** is a descriptive tool not an explanation. (See also the limitations of this tool on page 57.)

▶ Strengths of this project

◆ Data collection is easy and is readily available, and there is little danger involved in data collection. A wide variety of techniques can be used.

◆ The enquiry is locally-based and a small area yields excellent results.

◆ Most people have access to a shopping area or a small town.

◆ Accurate measurements can be made.

◆ There are a number of values and attitudes connected with the growth of peripheral shopping centres.

DELIMITING THE CBD

The **central business district (CBD)** is the commercial and economic core of cities. It is the heart of the city and the area which is most accessible to public transport. It has a number of characteristics:

♦ multi-storey development
 – high land values force buildings to grow upwards
 – the floor space of the CBD is much greater than the ground space

♦ concentration of retailing
 – accessibility attracts shops with high range and threshold characteristics
 – department stores dominate
 – specialist shops occupy less accessible areas

♦ public transport is concentrated in the CBD
 – there is a convergence of bus routes on the CBD

♦ offices are concentrated in the CBD
 – centrality favours office development

♦ vertical zoning is apparent
 – shops occupy ground floors
 – offices occupy upper floors

♦ few people live in the CBD
 – a few luxury flats exist
 – there may be some artisans, etc.

♦ pedestrian flows are highest in the CBD

♦ traffic restrictions are greatest in the CBD
 – pedestrianisation has reduced areas for cars since the 1960s.

▶ Hypotheses

♦ The CBD is the most accessible area of the city.

♦ Building heights increase in the CBD.

♦ Land use is mostly commercial – there is little residential or manufacturing land use.

♦ Pedestrian flows are greatest in the CBD.

♦ Parking restrictions increase in the CBD.

♦ Vertical zoning is apparent.

Photo 6.3 Traffic in Oxford – showing how routes converge on the city centre

▶ Techniques to be used

♦ A **flow diagram** of the city centre showing bus routes and their frequency (see page 42).

♦ A **line graph** for building height (see page 36).

♦ **Land-use mapping**.

♦ **Isolines** (contours) and **flow diagrams** showing changes in the level of pedestrian counts.

♦ A **map of parking restrictions**.

♦ **Pie charts** to compare ground-floor land use with upper-floor land uses (see page 38).

♦ **Simple descriptive statistics** such as percentages, maximum, minimum and trends can be used to good effect (see page 50).

Fig. 6.26 Land use in Oxford

Data collection methods

◆ Use a base map (such as *GOAD* map) to mark off an area which includes the CBD, and the area around it (it is important to have such an area as a contrast). Then using a pre-determined key, walk along each street (if the town is small) or selected streets (if it is very large) and record on the map (in the exact position) the following:
– height of the buildings, i.e. number of storeys (NB does it have a basement?)
– use of ground floor (e.g. commercial)
– use of upper floor (e.g. commercial, legal, financial, service)
– presence of traffic restrictions (e.g. parking metres, yellow lines, pedestrianised streets): interview a traffic warden, if you see one, to help you with this.

◆ Using bus timetables, gather data which shows the frequency and direction of bus routes.

◆ To test pedestrian flows, stand at a crossroads and record the number of people that pass by in a 15 minute period. Repeat this at a number of locations, radiating out from the CBD.

◆ The frontage of many CBD shops is indented, to increase display space. This can be easily measured by comparing the total window length against shop length.

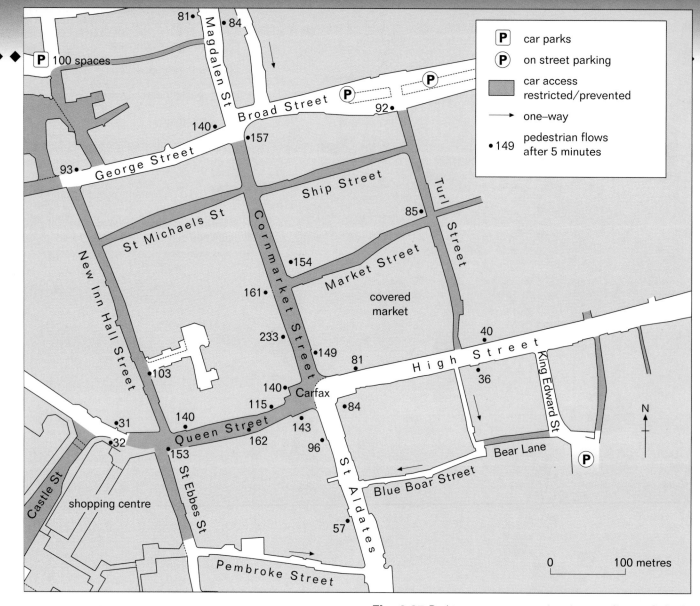

Fig. 6.27 Parking restrictions and pedestrian flow in Oxford

Fig. 6.28 (left) Bus routes converging on Oxford

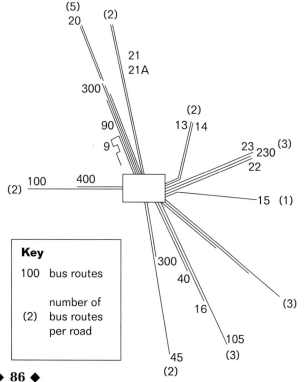

Key

100   bus routes

(2)   number of bus routes per road

▶ Presentation

The CBD is the most accessible part of town. The flow diagram (see Figure 6.28) shows the convergence of bus routes on the CBD: 23 routes meet there, one from as far away as Chipping Norton (26km away). All routes pass through the city centre. The next most accessible areas are Headington and Cowley.

Building heights increase towards the city centre. However, the highest building is only seven storeys high. This compares with two to three storeys outside the CBD. The reason for the high buildings in the CBD is the lack of space and huge land prices of the city centre. By building upwards developers can increase the floor space for each

Photo 6.4 Vertical zoning (1st floor: department store, 2nd floor: restaurant, 3rd-5th floor: solicitors)

area of ground. However, buildings in Oxford are not very high – this is due to the city's architectural heritage and planning restrictions on the height that buildings can reach.

The land-use map (see Figure 6.26) shows that in the area surrounding Carfax (the central crossroads in Oxford), the majority of activities (71%) are commercial, followed by other services (25%) and educational/cultural (4%). Residential is higher than expected (2%), due to the presence of colleges, but there is little manufacturing. These can be shown on a pie chart.

Pedestrian flows are greatest at Cornmarket (about 200 per five minutes) and tail off rapidly away from the CBD. Readings at Gloucester Green (93) and Magdalen Street (81) illustrate the sharp fall in the number of pedestrians.

The map of parking restrictions (see Figure 6.27) shows that there are parking restrictions and restricted access throughout the CBD. There are

only two areas of parking close to the CBD, and cars are prohibited from most of the streets.

In Cornmarket (the main shopping street) ground-floor cover was dominated by commercial enterprises (71%) but first-floor activities were more varied. Other services (e.g. legal and financial) covered 14% and restaurants 9%. Look at Photo 6.4 which shows vertical zoning in the CBD (the ground floor is used by a department store, the next floor used for a restaurant and the top three floors are used by a firm of solicitors).

Shops in the CBD characteristically had a window length/shop length of 1, but shops outside the CBD had a ratio of 1 or under.

▶ Limitations of this project

◆ Pedestrian flows:
  – it is impossible to record all places at the same time
  – pedestrian flows vary day-by-day, and seasonally.

◆ CBDs are tourist centres.

◆ It may be difficult to find out functions on the upper floors and whether the building contains a basement.

◆ Other forms of transport bring people to the CBD (e.g. cars, trains, bike, walk).

◆ It is also difficult to classify functions (e.g. Marks and Spencer's contains a food hall and a restaurant as well as its retail function).

▶ Strengths of this project

◆ It allows a wide range of data to be collected.

◆ The data can be collected quite easily.

◆ Many techniques can be used.

◆ CBDs are easy to get to.

◆ It allows a particular CBD to be compared with a model one.

◆ Most candidates are familiar with their local CBD.

◆ There are many values, attitudes and judgements (e.g. feelings about congestion, pedestrianisation, etc.).

MICROCLIMATE AROUND THE SCHOOL

Some classrooms are always cold, others are blinding with the sun streaming in through the windows. Snow and ice remain longer on some areas. What can we learn from simple tests around the school and its playing fields that will teach us about small-scale changes in climate?

Hypotheses

◆ Rainfall varies around the school due to:
  – vegetation
  – obstructions (e.g. walls, buildings, etc.).

◆ North-facing places are colder than south-facing places (i.e. aspect).

◆ Contrasts are most noticeable in winter.

◆ Changes throughout the day occur in areas of differing vegetation and aspect.

Techniques

◆ **Isolines** to show variations in rainfall in a small area (see page 43).

◆ **Dispersion diagrams** to compare different results for different areas (see page 46).

◆ **Simple descriptive statistics** (i.e. mean, mode and median) to describe data (see page 50).

◆ **Line graphs** to compare temperature between north- and south-facing slopes over the course of a day (see page 36).

◆ **Land-use mapping** to show contrasts in vegetation and site characteristics.

Data collection methods

Map out the areas to be used. Different areas may be used to test different hypotheses.

For example, an exposed flat roof (often the top of a science block) can be used to check rainfall variability in a small area. Using at least a dozen rain gauges, place them in contrasting locations: next to a wall, an exposed site, close to a grill, on the east and west sides (or north and south) of an obstruction, and so on. Record the rainfall totals in each gauge clearly.

Photo 6.5 Recording rainfall under evergreen shrubs

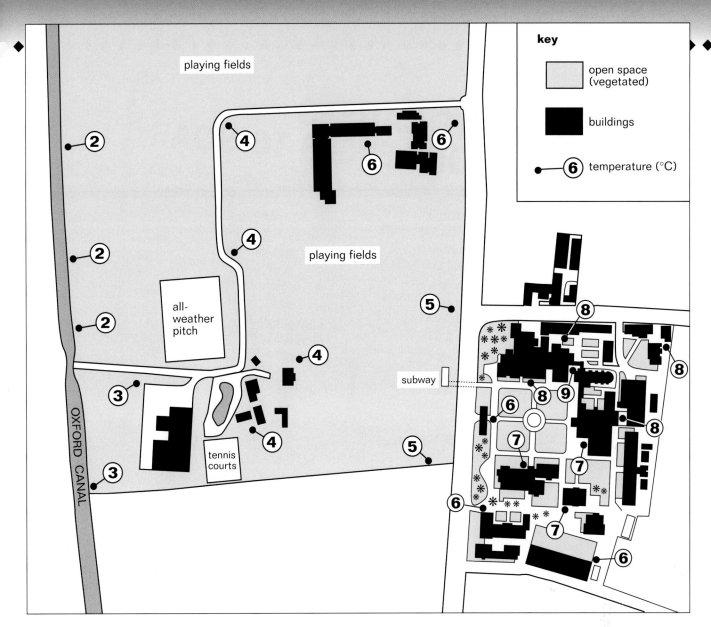

Fig. 6.29 The heat island effect: minimum temperatures recorded during high pressure conditions (November 1995)

Place rain gauges in the school grounds in areas of different vegetation – close to rose bushes, deciduous vegetation, coniferous vegetation, grass and shrubs. You will need at least five rain gauges in each area. This experiment shows whether the type and density of vegetation effects the amount of interception of rainfall.

Maximum and minimum thermometers can be placed on north- and south-facing walls and also in areas of different vegetation types. Maximum and minimum temperatures should be recorded each day.

Temperature varies throughout the day with vegetation and aspect. Temperatures should be recorded hourly so that an accurate picture can be built up of microclimate around the school.

▶ Presentation

Most of the rain gauges on the flat roof of a science block (75%) recorded 16–17mm of rain. However, five gauges recorded lower amounts. Two gauges placed behind a small wall recorded only 8 and 9mm of rain; two close to a small obstruction recorded 12 and 14mm, and the fifth gauge by the entrance recorded 12mm. The isolines drawn (lines of equal value, in this case rainfall) showed that rainfall decreases close to an obstruction. The bigger the obstruction the greater the difference.

Rainfall varied with vegetation type (see Figure 6.31). The five gauges under coniferous vegetation had an average of 1·5mm; and the deciduous vegetation 15mm, open grass 17mm, shrubs

HEATWAVE CAUSES POLLUTION LEVELS TO SOAR

Ozone levels in Oxford and the surrounding areas exceeded the World Health Organisation's safe limits this week in Oxford. Oxford City Council's pollution monitoring station recorded six hours of poor air quality on 31st July, and nine hours on each of August 1st and 2nd. The City Council has urged drivers not to go into the city centre unless it was necessary and has warned asthmatics, anyone with respiratory disorders and the elderly to avoid strenuous exercise. In places such as Oxford, the high levels of exhaust fumes concentrated in such a small area create high levels of carbon monoxide and nitrogen oxides. In addition, ozone is created by the sun reacting with the fumes given off by cars. Under high pressure conditions, with little wind, the problem is intensified as the pollutants remain in the area. Low pressure systems blow the pollutants away, so the problem is very much linked with the hot, sunny weather that we normally get in the summer.

Fig. 6.30 Newspaper report (based on reports in the *Oxford Times* between May and Aug., 1995)

6–7mm and the rose garden 15mm. The dispersion diagram show the contrasts very clearly.

Temperature contrasts between north- and south-facing walls were not very great. North-facing walls reached -4°C and south-facing walls reached -3°C. By contrast, walls close to the school boiler only dropped to 2°C, and ice and snow was not recorded over the winter months.

The greater contrast was in the daily variation. South-facing walls began to heat up at about 9am, but the north-facing walls were still below freezing at 11am. Only by 3pm had the north-facing walls caught up with (and overtaken) the south-facing walls. It was dark by 4.30pm.

▶ Limitations of this project

◆ It is important to stress external factors, the climate in the school is very much affected by much larger-scale climatic factors.

◆ Quite heavy rainfall is needed for the best results.

◆ A good range of vegetation types is also desirable.

◆ It is very time-consuming measuring temperature hourly.

◆ The best contrast in temperature is in the early morning (minimum night-time temperatures) and during cold winter spells.

◆ External conditions will effect results. It is crucial that there are taken into account when explaining results.

▶ Strengths of this project

◆ It is very local in the scale.

◆ It is very easy to set up.

◆ Measurements are very accurate.

◆ It can form part of a group or class exercise.

◆ It helps our understanding about climatic patterns on a larger scale (e.g. alpine valleys and aspect, vegetation and humidity).

◆ It helps us to understand why forests are planted to prevent soil erosion. How do they reduce soil erosion?

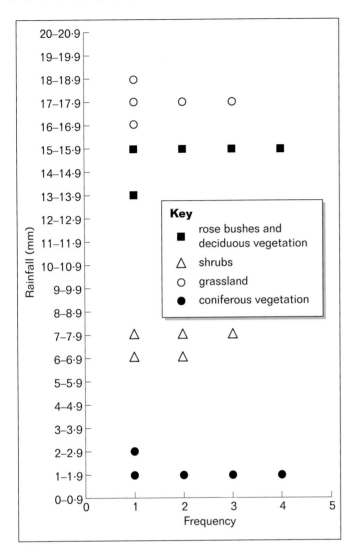

Fig. 6.31 Dispersion diagram to show variation of rainfall totals in rain gauges under different types of vegetation

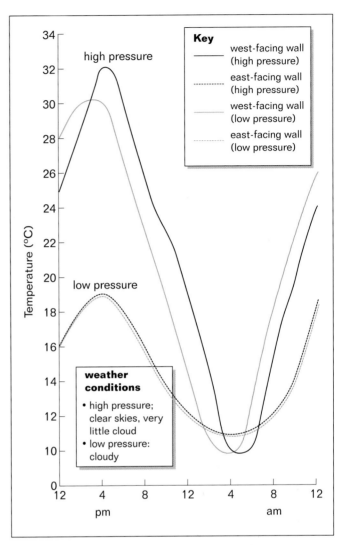

Fig. 6.32 Daily (diurnal) temperature variations on east- and west-facing walls during high pressure and low pressure conditions

FOOTPATH EROSION

Dramatic photographs of areas suffering desertification are quite common now. Much of this has been caused by overgrazing and trampling by herds of animals around boreholes. Less important, but equally visible, are the severely eroded footpaths that lead up to the summits of Snowdonia and Red Tarn. Tourist 'honey spots' bare the scars of excessive use. We can observe this process at a much more local scale by analysing footpath erosion.

Hypotheses

◆ There is more erosion at the centre of a footpath.

◆ Soil and moisture content and organic content increase away from the centre of a footpath.

◆ Vegetation height, type, diversity and density increase away from the footpath.

◆ The level of impact varies with the number of people using the path.

Techniques

◆ A **cross-section** to show small-scale variations in relief (see page 8).

◆ A **scattergraph** (see page 37) and a line of best fit to show variations in moisture and organic content with distance from the footpath. **Spearman's rank correlation coeffecient** (see page 54) to test whether there is a relationship between variables and distance from the centre of the footpath. **Triangular graphs** (see page 47) to show variations in the composition of the soil.

◆ **Pie charts**, **line-graphs** and **kite diagrams** (see pages 36 and 38) for plant species, height, density and diversity with distance from footpath.

◆ **Flow diagrams** (see page 42) to show variations in pedestrian flow.

Data collection methods

◆ Choose two contrasting footpaths, one that is well-used and one that is less heavily used. Using a linear sample (called a **transect**, see page 64) take samples from the centre of the footpath and at metre intervals up to a distance of 5m either side of the path (see Figure 6.33).

Photo 6.6 Gulleying caused by trampling, Shotover

◆ To record variations in relief on the footpath use a tape and a metre rule, and measure the depth to which the footpath has been eroded at 10cm regular intervals.

◆ Take a sample of soil with a soil auger if possible or, if not, use a small trowel. Place about a handful of soil in an airtight bag. To measure moisture content weigh a sample of soil (S_1). Place it in an oven and burn it at 100°C for twenty-four hours. Reweigh the sample (S_2).

To work out the moisture content of the sample use a formula:

$$\frac{S_1 - S_2}{S_1} \times 100\%$$

To work out organic content take the sample S_2 and burn it over a bunsen burner at maximum heat for 15 minutes. Reweigh the burned sample (S_3), and the organic content is found by using the formula:

$$\frac{S_2 - S_3}{S_2} \times 100\%$$

◆ To measure percentage vegetation cover, use a quadrat and count the number of squares which are covered by bare ground and each type of vegetation. Vegetation type can be identified by use of a plant guide. Diversity refers to the number of different types of species present, and height can be measured by a metre rule, or for trees by estimating. An accurate way to measure the height of trees is to use a 45° set square. View along the longest edge, line up the top of the tree, measure the distance from where you are standing to the tree, add this to your height from ground level to eye level, and this gives you the height of the tree (see Figure 6.34).

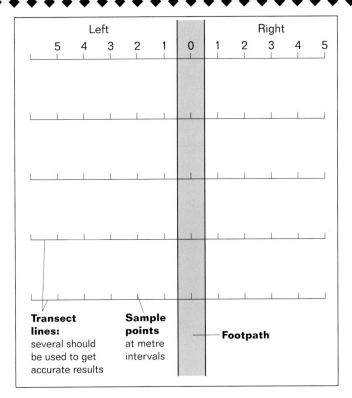

Fig. 6.33 Transect across a footpath to show study points

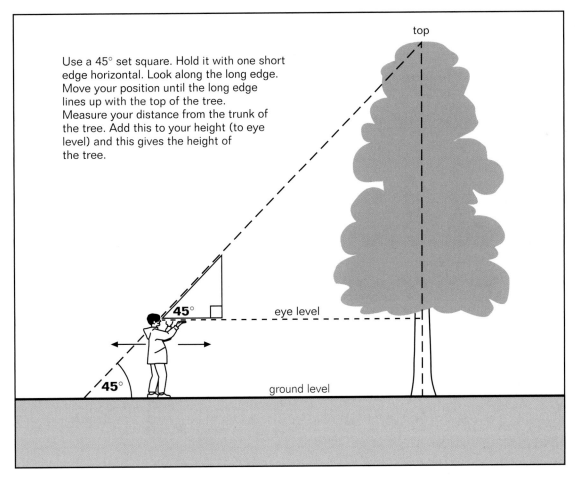

Use a 45° set square. Hold it with one short edge horizontal. Look along the long edge. Move your position until the long edge lines up with the top of the tree. Measure your distance from the trunk of the tree. Add this to your height (to eye level) and this gives the height of the tree.

Fig. 6.34 Estimating the height of trees

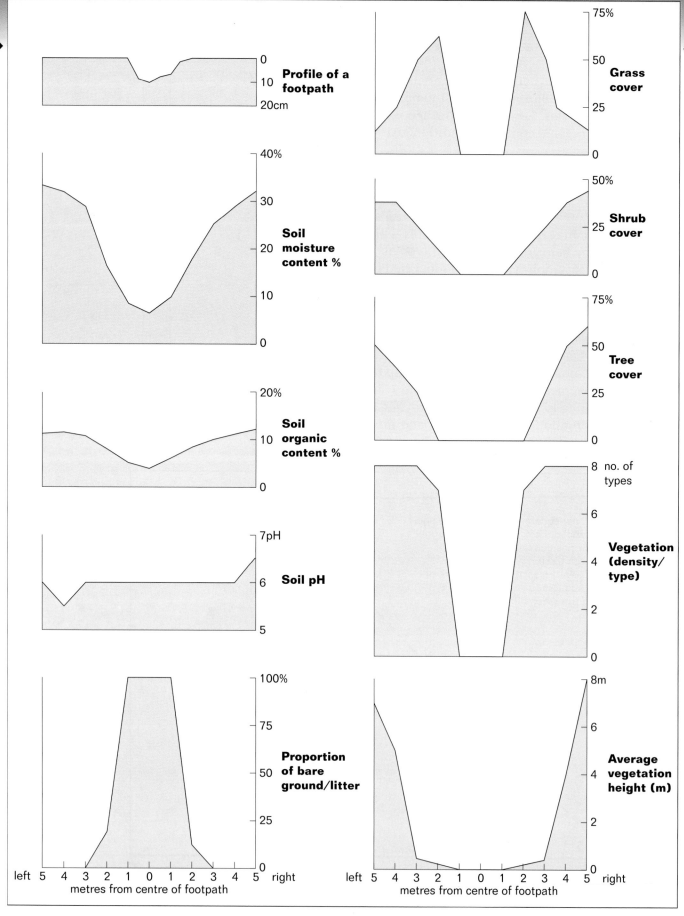

Fig. 6.35 Variations in cross-section, soil and vegetation characteristics across a heavily-used footpath

- Count the number of people (and the amount of litter) that use the path in a given period of time. These can be divided into groups. Families with young children, elderly people with dogs, joggers, cyclists, horse riders, etc. The impact will vary with the activity involved.

Presentation

There is strong evidence that footpath erosion is widespread on the paths at Shotover (see Photo 6.6). The cross-section shows in Figure 6.35 how deeply pitted the surface is, and small gullies have been formed up to a depth of 12cm. When it rains, water flows over these and erodes the path even further. The gullies are deepest in the centre and more pronounced in the well-used paths.

Analysis of the soil shows that both organic and moisture content increase with distance from the centre. Moisture content rises from 7% in the centre, to 33% five metres away: the trend is quite striking. Similarly organic content rises from 3·5% to 12%. Both of these results were tested using Spearman's rank correlation coefficient: the results were 95% significant. There is also a strong correlation between organic content and moisture content: as organic content increases so too does moisture content. This is found to be also 95% significant. As the vegetation cover provides shade it reduces the temperature of the soil, thereby reducing evaporation. Consequently, soil moisture and organic content are related. The strength of this relationship depends upon the type and density of vegetation, as well as the seasonality and amount of water present.

Distinct vegetation changes were apparent. The percentage of bare ground decreased away from the footpath centre, while the height of the vegetation and the density of the vegetation increased. Diversity varied, in some cases a tree dominated the site, and consequently there was less light available for ground plants. The pie charts clearly show variations in the type and intensive use of the two paths. One path (which was a bridleway) was used regularly by dog walkers, horseriders, orienteers and cyclists, whereas the other path was used only by individuals and couples out walking.

Limitations of this project

- Erosion is a long-term process. The project does not necessarily show current processes.
- Soil augers are expensive and many schools do not have them.
- It is not easy to identify vegetation, especially if it is not in flower.
- It is not always possible to measure each side of a footpath (e.g. consider a footpath that runs through a field – the farmer would not like soil samples to be taken up to 5m away from the centre of the path).
- Laboratory work requires supervision.

Strengths of this project

- A small area yields excellent results.
- A wide range of techniques and methods can be used.
- Measurements are accurate and scientifically worked out.
- Comparisons can be made between different areas, different rock types, different intensities of land use, etc.
- There is a strong 'values' section – why people like a particular area, why a particular footpath is very popular, etc.
- It links physical and human geography.
- It raises issues about management.

WATER QUALITY

Water pollution of rivers, streams and lakes occurs in both rural and urban areas. Sources of pollution can be organic matter such as sewage, leaf litter, food waste or farm effluent. The matter is decomposed by bacteria and fungi, which take up oxygen from the water for their aerobic respiration – this may reduce oxygen concentrations to a level where some species of aquatic life cannot survive. Nitrate pollution from fertiliser runoff, and phosphates from sewage and detergents, leads to eutrophication whereby algae and surface plants (e.g. like duckweed) thrive at the expense of other organisms.

▶ Hypotheses

You could select two ponds or rivers for comparison, one polluted and the other unpolluted. Alternatively, find a river, stream or canal with a sewage works, effluent outflow or area of intensive farming. Your hypotheses might be based on one or more of the following.

◆ Animal species will change with respect to different oxygen levels in the water and possible sources of pollution.

◆ Pollution levels will decrease with distance downstream from the source of the pollution, i.e. the river will 'recover'.

◆ Well-oxygenated freshwater rivers, streams and ponds will support a wider range of animal species than poorly-oxygenated water bodies.

▶ Safety

Choose sites on the river bank which are safe to work from, and where there is good access to water. Always use rubber gloves as a protection against infection. Bacteria from sewage and Weil's disease (*leptospiral* jaundice) are real dangers. During hot weather, blooms of blue-green algae may appear on the surface – these can cause skin irritation.

▶ Data collection methods

The methods outlined here are quick and cheap to use, and provide adequate data for a comparative study.

◆ A five-minute **kick sample** to identify animal species. The river bed is disturbed by kicking material into a net and animal species are then identified using a biotic index.

◆ **Water temperature** is measured directly with an electronic thermometer.

◆ **Ion concentrations** (e.g. nitrates, phosphates, chlorides and ammonium) can be measured using HACH test kits which are sold by Camlab in the UK.

◆ **Dissolved oxygen** is measured using an oxygen meter, this measures the dissolved oxygen at site. The meter should not be placed directly in the stream, as air bubbles form on the membrane giving false readings.

◆ **Biological oxygen demand, BOD$_5$** (the amount of oxygen consumed in a sample of water over a period of five days in the dark at 20°C) is compared to dissolved oxygen content taken in the field – the difference is the BOD.

◆ The **pH** level is measured with a pH probe.

◆ **Velocity of stream** is measured using a flow meter.

◆ **Detergent** is found by half filling a clear sample bottle, shaking it and recording how long it takes the froth to clear.

◆ **Observation** – signs of pollution are dead fish, foam, oil, discolouration, bad smell.

◆ **Land-use mapping** can be carried out along the whole stretch of river, making note of residential, industrial and agricultural land-use. In agricultural areas, try to get details from farms as to when fertilisers are applied.

◆ **Recording** heavy rain or periods of drought can also be useful.

Each of these measures is simple and the equipment is relatively cheap. However, costs will soon build up, so select three or four of the tests which best suit your hypotheses.

Class of waterway	Fauna	Biochemical oxygen demand (mg O_2 absorbed per litre of water at 20°C in 5 days)	Waterway used for:
I	Diverse; salmon, trout, grayling, stonefly and mayfly nymphs, caddis larvae, *Gammarus*.	0–3	Domestic supply
II	Trout rarely dominant; chub, dace, caddis larvae, *Gammarus*.	4–10 (increased in summer at times of low flow)	Agriculture. Industrial processes
III	Roach, gudgeon, *Asellus*; mayfly nymphs and caddis larvae rare.	11–15	Irrigation
IV	Fish absent. Red chirinimid larvae (bloodworms) and *Tubifex* worms present.	16–30 (completely deoxygenated from time to time).	Very little. Unsuitable for amenity use
V	Barren, or with fungus or small *Tubifex* worms.	>30	None

(Adapted from D.H. Mills, *An Introduction to Freshwater Biology*, Oliver and Boyd, 1972)

Fig. 6.36 Freshwater animals as indicators of pollution

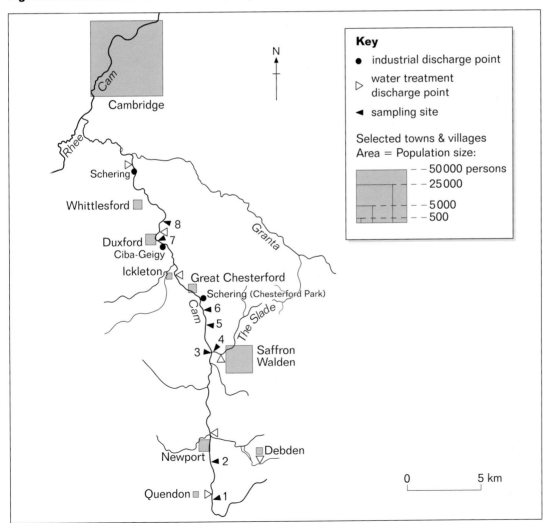

Fig. 6.37 Sampling a large stretch of river

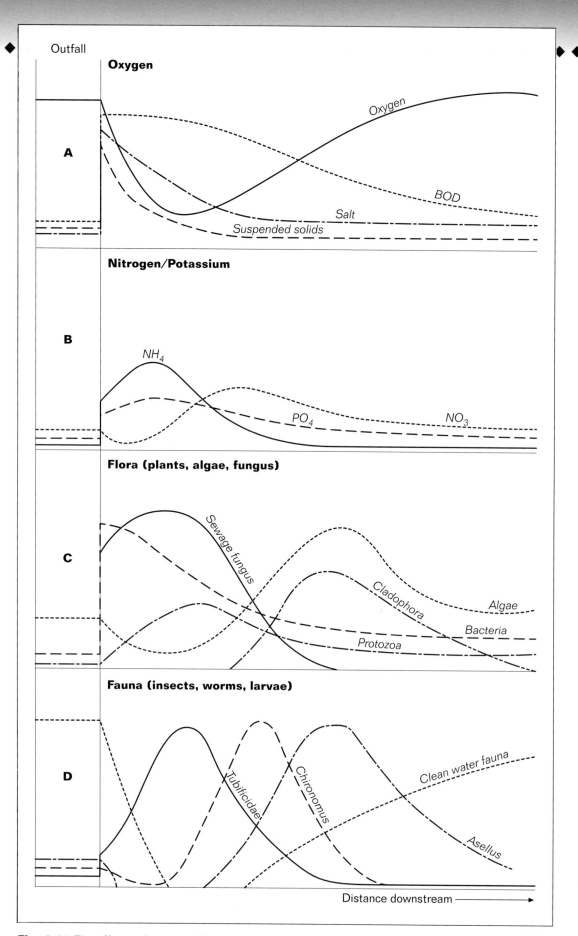

Fig. 6.38 The effects of organic effluent upon a river at the outfall and downstream

▶ Techniques

All the measures must be mapped and related to the different sample sites along the river. The simplest method is by using one or a series of annotated sketch maps, using pie or bar charts and proportional circles to illustrate pollution levels (see pages 38 and 40). Simple line graphs can also be used effectively (see Figure 6.38).

Scattergraphs (see page 37) are used to correlate different variables (e.g. BOD and species diversity). The use of simple statistics like Spearman's rank correlation coefficient (see page 54) are also helpful in supporting findings.

▶ Presentation

Figure 6.36 shows the link between freshwater animals and levels of pollution. Classes IV and V are heavily polluted and, clearly, the river's tolerance has been exceeded in these stages.

Figure 6.38 shows the way a river might recover with distance from a source of pollution, in this case, a sewage outfall.

▶ Limitations of this project

◆ Polluted rivers are smelly and often dangerous (see section on safety page 96).

◆ Some sites are inaccessible, so this makes random sampling difficult.

◆ Results can be affected by local weather conditions. Drought followed by heavy rain can lead to pollutants being flushed into the river, giving above normal levels; conversely, if the drought is prolonged, your river might dry up!

◆ The equipment needed for easy testing can be very expensive in total.

▶ Strengths of this project

◆ River pollution is a serious environmental concern and there is a chance for the researcher to determine the real effects of land use.

◆ The investigation lends itself to both urban and rural water sites at a variety of scales.

◆ The wide variety of techniques means there is considerable flexibility of approach.

SAND DUNES

Sand dunes represent a dynamic environment for a number of highly specialised plants and animals. There is an ecological relationship between the shape of the dunes and the type of plants. The influence of human activities is also very important. The vegetation on sand dunes is easily destroyed by the constant trampling of walkers, exposing sand which is quickly removed by wind, resulting in 'blow-outs' and 'gulleying'. Other aspects of the human impact on dunes include water and fire hazard, created in the dry summer months by cigarettes and barbecues.

▶ Hypotheses

This investigation links the change in size and environmental conditions of dunes with distance inland, to the succession of plant species. Figure 6.39 shows these changes. We can derive the following hypotheses from this diagram.

- ◆ The further inland you travel the more diverse a selection of plant species will be found, until a climax community is reached after which diversity will decline.
- ◆ Soil acidity will increase with distance inland.

Fig. 6.39 The dynamic dune environment

- ◆ Organic content will increase with distance inland.
- ◆ Freshwater content will increase with distance inland.
- ◆ There will be a series of dunes: starting with a small embryo dune, followed by a larger fore dune, then the largest dune and the first dune ridge.

▶ Data collection methods

The data collection for this investigation involves four different approaches. (See page 63 for sampling.)

- ◆ **Profiling:** use ranging poles, a clinometer and a measuring tape to measure the profile of the sand dunes. Begin at the driftwood line on the beach and measure to each break of slope (or at 10m intervals) using the clinometer to measure gradient (see Figure 6.40).
- ◆ **Quadrats:** use a 0·25m quadrat to estimate the percentage vegetation cover and diversity of plant species. Sites should be selected at the break of slope and/or at measured intervals. Vegetation height can also be measured. A classification of sand dune plants should be used to aid identification.

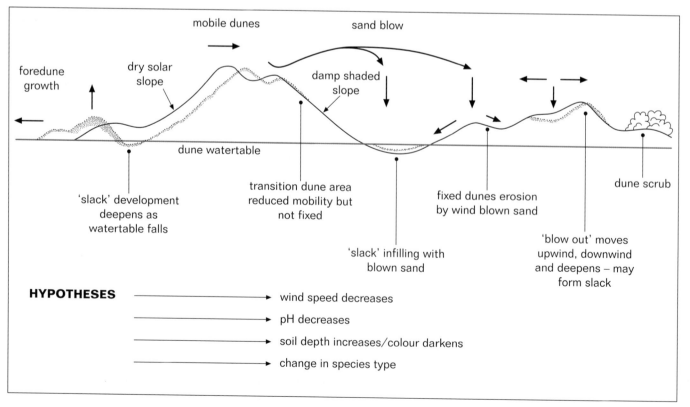

- **Soil tests:** soil samples should be taken where vegetation is measured. Take soil from a depth of 15cm and seal it in a small, clearly-labelled plastic bag. Once back at school, use an oven to measure soil water and soil organic content:
  - **soil water content:** weigh the sample and dry it overnight at 10°C and then reweigh
  $\dfrac{\text{weight loss on drying}}{\text{weight of wet soil}} \times 100\% = \%$ water (by weight) contained in the soil
  - **soil organic content:** the sample is then heated for 20–30 minutes over a full-flame bunsen burner and, when cool, is reweighed
  $\dfrac{\text{weight loss on burning}}{\text{weight of dry soil}} \times 100\% = \%$ organic matter (by weight) of dry soil
  - **soil acidity:** this can be found in the field or in the lab. A small sample of soil (from 15cm depth) is placed in a tube with barium sulphate and universal indicator solution. The colour change is recorded and compared to a ready-made chart. (Alternatively, a shop bought pH test kit can be purchased from any garden shop.)

- **Microclimate**
  - temperature and humidity can be measured using a wet and dry bulb hygrometer
  - windspeed can be measured using an anemometer.

▶ Techniques

- The **slope profile** should be drawn on graph paper, and on this cross-section you should identify the following in each sample site:
  - changes in slope shape (component profile)
  - changes in vegetation type (succession)
  - pH; soil moisture and content
  - wind speed and humidity.

- **Kite diagrams** are an interesting way of displaying information about vegetation. Use a percentage scale to show the change in vegetation over distance (see Figure 6.42). You can link these figures to other plant species (e.g. dandelion; thistle; holly; gorse). You can also link a particular plant type to another measure (e.g. pH, windspeed, aspect) by adding that below the kite.

- **Line graphs** and **scattergraphs** can be used to correlate different variables (see Figure 6.43)

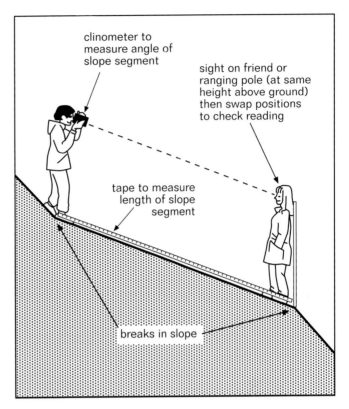

Fig. 6.40 Profiling using a clinometer

Fig. 6.41 Significance test for the percentage water loss and organic matter (using Spearman's rank correlation coefficient)

Site	Water matter	Rank	Organic	Rank	d	d²
1	0·3	11	0·2	14	−3	9
3	0·08	14	0·3	12	2	4
5	0·07	13	0·2	14	−1	1
6	0·07	13	0·3	12	1	1
7	1·8	5	0·4	10	−5	25
9	0·08	14	0·4	10	4	16
10	0·44	10	0·7	8	2	4
13	8·4	1	1	7	−6	36
16	0·2	12	2	5	7	49
18	1·6	6	0·7	8	−2	4
19	5·2	2	5	2	0	0
21	0·6	9	0·5	9	0	0
24	2·6	4	3	3	1	1
27	1·4	7	2	5	2	4
29	1·2	8	3	3	5	25
30	5	3	1	1	2	4
						183

$n = 16$ $d^2 = 183$ $6\sum d^2 = 1098$

$1 - \dfrac{1098}{4096 - 16} = 0.7308823$ **strong positive correlation**

Significance $0.05 = 0.425$
Significance $0.01 = 0.601$ **99% significance**

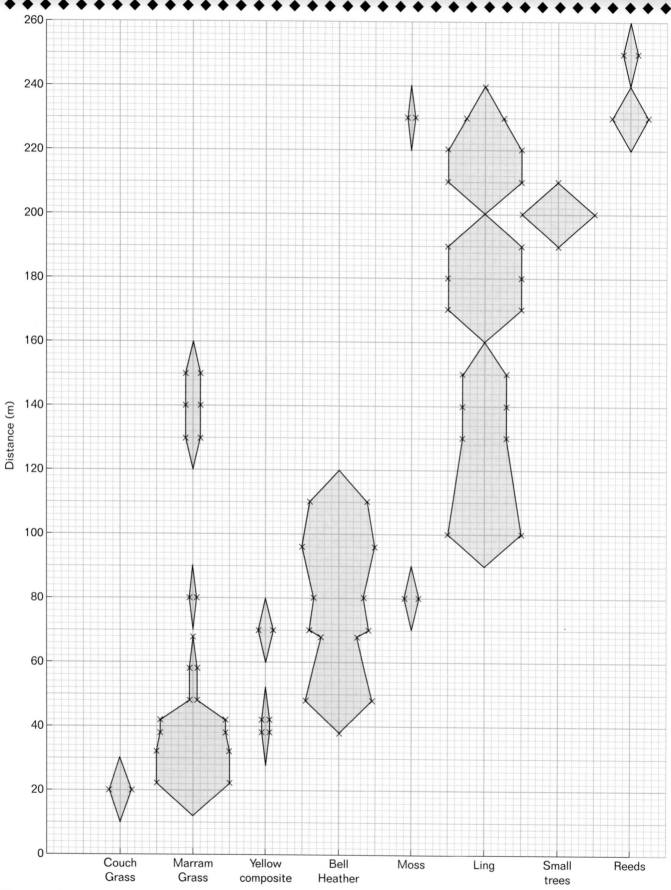

Fig. 6.42 Kite diagrams from a transect along dunes in Studland Bay, Dorset

Presentation

Figure 6.43 is a simple line graph comparing soil moisture content with organic matter from the Holkham sand dunes in Norfolk. Spearman's rank coefficient revealed a correlation of 0·73, a very strong positive correlation.

Figure 6.42 shows kite diagrams from a transect along dunes in Studland Bay, Dorset. The succession from grasses to trees and shrubs is very clear.

Limitations of this project

◆ A certain amount of specialised and fairly expensive equipment is needed for this investigation.

◆ Human impact can fundamentally alter the dune transect – this must be accounted for.

◆ Dune species are best identified when in flower, so spring and summer are the best times for surveying.

◆ Profiling needs at least two people.

◆ Official clearance is needed to work on some dunes.

Strengths of this project

◆ The study can be carried out over a small area.

◆ The beach setting makes this an ideal investigation to be carried in the summer holidays.

◆ An excellent variety of data can be obtained.

◆ A large number of techniques can be used with a number of different methods of presentation relevant.

Fig. 6.43 Soil moisture content and organic matter in the Holkham sand dunes, Norfolk

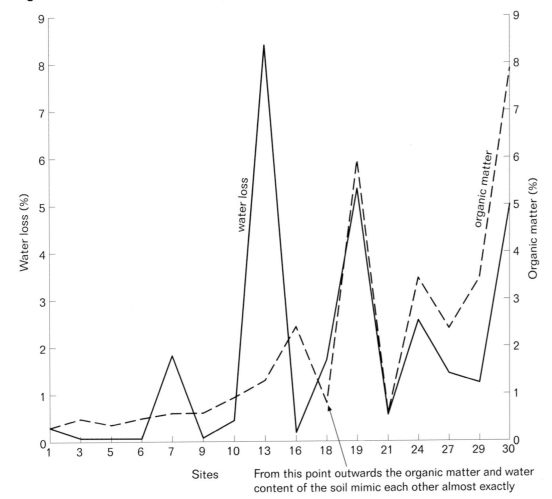

Sites

From this point outwards the organic matter and water content of the soil mimic each other almost exactly

CRITICAL

CRIME

Are there parts of a town that you would rather not go to alone or at night? Where are these areas, and why don't you want to go there? The geography of crime is a fascinating topic. The type and rate of criminal activity varies with settlement size, within different parts of an urban area, and with a variety of geographic factors (such as land use, population density, housing type and physical geography). The amount of crime also varies in rural areas, with larger settlements reporting more crimes than smaller ones.

▶ Hypotheses

◆ The type and number of crimes reported varies within urban areas.

◆ Crime is associated with certain geographic factors.

◆ Levels of crime vary with size of settlement.

▶ Techniques

To test the hypothesis that the type and number of crimes reported varies within urban areas, you would use:

◆ **choropleth maps** showing levels of crime within an urban area (see page 44)

Photo 6.7 A burnt out car, Blackbird Leys, Oxford

◆ **proportional divided pie-charts** to show how crime varies from area to area (see page 38)

◆ **statistics** (e.g. percentages, maximum and minimum) to describe the patterns and level of crime (see page 50).

To test the hypothesis that crime is associated with certain geographic factors, you would use:

◆ **scattergraphs** and a line of best fit to show the relationship between the level of crime and geographic factor(s) (see page 37)

◆ **simple statistics** to describe any relationship (e.g. maximum, minimum, trend and exception) and statistical tests (e.g. Spearman's rank correlation) to test for statistical significance

◆ **maps of geographic factors**, e.g. distribution of car parks, shops, unemployment.

To test the hypothesis that levels of crime vary with size of settlement, you would use:

◆ **scattergraphs** and line of best fit

◆ **proportional divided pie-charts** to show how crime varies from area to area

◆ **statistics** (e.g. percentages, maximum and minimum) to describe the patterns and level of crime.

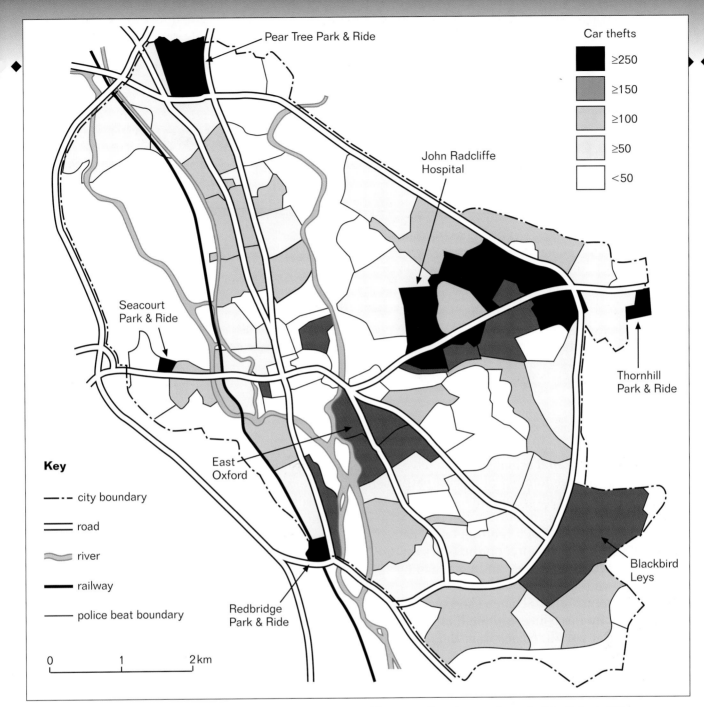

Fig. 6.44 Distribution of car theft in Oxford, 1994

▶ Data collection methods

For the hypothesis that the 'type and number of crimes reported varies with urban areas', you would use the following.

◆ **Police data**: the data relating to crime are readily available from the statistical department of most police forces. These distinguish between different types of crime, such as robbery, car theft, burglary and shoplifting. The data are reported for police 'beat' areas, allowing a detailed picture to be drawn. In some cases a beat map is not available – this can easily be constructed by using a beat index and a local road map.

◆ **Local newspapers**: the local press reports most serious incidents, but not minor ones. By checking the papers over a period of at least one month it is possible to see which crimes are being reported, and where they occur. This can be compared with similar data from the police.

◆ **Magistrate and Crown Court reports**: this is very time consuming, as only a small fraction of crimes are dealt with on a daily basis in the courts. However, it provides much valuable information, not just about the crime but also about defendants and their backgrounds. It is rather like a detailed case study.

Drug addicts top Oxford's crime league

HEROIN USERS ACCOUNT FOR 60% OF CITY THEFTS 60 per cent of all burglars and robbers in Oxford are heroin addicts.

The astonishing statistic highlights the increasing problem caused by drug abuse in the city.

Chief Superintendent Ralph Perry, the man in charge of Oxford's police force, is partly blaming the growing spread of drugs on what he calls 'the huge transient population in east Oxford'.

Police statistics show that there were 5,228 burglaries and robberies in 1995 in the Oxford police area, and Mr. Perry said 'Research has shown that 60% of our burglars have a serious opiate habit.'

Addicts must steal £100,000 worth of goods to be able to afford enough heroin for a year.

'One of the features of Oxford is that we have a huge transient population and I don't think that helps.

He pointed to the large number of rented houses in the east Oxford area as a breeding ground for drug addicts, but he refused to blame students for the problem.

(Source: *The Oxford Times*, July 12th, 1996)

Fig. 6.45 Drug addicts top Oxford's crime league (newspaper extract)

◆ **Neighbourhood watch schemes:** these have developed in a large number of places, partly as a response to rising levels of crime and partly as a means of preventing crime. An interview with the Neighbourhood Watch representative can provide a lot of information on the types of crime that occur in an area, and what can be done to prevent this. Data from the Neighbourhood Watch Scheme can be compared with data from the police, although much of their data (but not all) comes from the police.

For the hypothesis that 'crime is associated with certain geographic factors', you would use the following.

◆ **The census:** a census is a population count which provides a great deal of statistical data about the characteristics of a population. The latest census (taken in 1991) can be used to show geographic variations in employment levels, housing type, ethnicity, age of population and so on. It is available in most central public libraries and on CD-Rom.

◆ **Environmental survey**: this enables the student to investigate the conditions of the surroundings (ranging from graffiti, litter and dirt), to the provision of facilities (such as recreation amenities and the safety of an area, levels of traffic, and derelict buildings). A **housing quality index** is also useful and provides a comparison with the statistical analysis of the census. Although these surveys are subjective (since people's views will vary as to what is good or bad), if it is carried out in a number of places by the same person it allows meaningful comparisons to be made.

◆ **Distribution of car parks:** the City Council transport department can provide data on the number of car parking spaces and their location. This can be compared to the distribution of car theft. Remember that it is important to consider other types of car parks (e.g. those at hospital, those in the workplace).

◆ **Number and distribution of shops:** land-use surveys of shopping areas will provide data on the number and types of shops in a number of areas (such as the CBD, secondary centres, neighbourhood shopping parades, etc.). These can be compared with the rates of shoplifting. Interviews with shop managers and shopping centre managers may produce information on security, the use of close-circuit televisions, etc.

For the hypothesis that 'levels of crime vary with size of settlement', you would use the following.

◆ As above for levels and types of crime.

◆ **Census** – for population size.

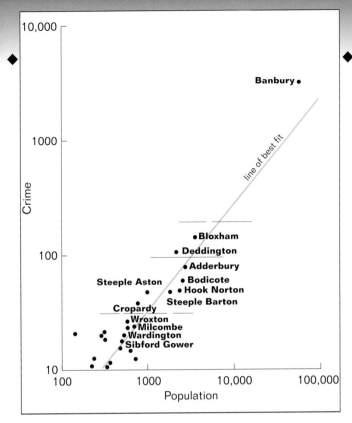

Fig. 6.46 Settlement size and the amount of reported crime

▶ Presentation

Vehicle theft is widespread around Oxford (see Figure 6.44). Vehicle theft includes: theft of cars, vans, mopeds and motorcycles etc.; theft of parts from the vehicle; attempted theft. In 1994, over 6,000 cases of vehicle theft were recorded by the police (over 25% of all crimes recorded in Oxford). The pattern shows a concentration in the Headington area of Oxford and to a lesser extent around the central area, parts of East Oxford, Blackbird Leys, the University and North Oxford near the Pear Tree 'park and ride' car park.

A number of factors can be suggested to explain this pattern: the location of car parks, hospitals, centres of employment and (in the case of Blackbird Leys and to a lesser extent Lower Wolvercote) areas where joyriding is not uncommon. Data relating to car theft is more reliable than for other crimes because car-insurance claims demand that thefts are reported to the police (if they are not reported, the victim could not make a claim on the insurance policy). However, while theft of vehicles is largely reported, theft from vehicles is not.

In general, as settlement size increases so too does the number of reported crimes. For example, Cropardy with a population of about 700 had just over 40 crimes reported, whereas Bloxham with a population of about 3,000 had nearly 200 crimes reported. However, Steeple Aston (population 1,000) and Hook Norton (population 2,000) each had a similar level of reported crime: 50. We can test if this is statistically significant by using the Spearman's rank correlation (see page 54) for a detailed explanation of the test). Putting the figures in we get a result 0·65, which tells us that we can be 95% sure that there is a significant relationship between population size and the number of reported crimes. The next step is to suggest reasons why population size influences the amount of reported crime.

▶ Limitations of this project

- ◆ Not all crimes are reported to the police.

- ◆ Data for car theft and burglary are more reliable as they are reported for insurance claims.

- ◆ The police beat areas are not always the same as the census ward areas.

- ◆ A correlation between crime and ethnic minorities, or crime and students, does not mean that the ethnic minority or the students are the criminals. They may be the victims or there might not be any connection.

- ◆ Data for the census dates from 1991; crime data is available for 1996, and survey data is the most up-to-date.

- ◆ Some areas are dangerous and should be avoided.

▶ Strengths of this project

- ◆ Clear geographic patterns exist.

- ◆ It is a fascinating topic.

- ◆ There is a range of primary and secondary data available.

- ◆ It can help a Neighbourhood Watch Scheme.

- ◆ It allows many graphic, cartographic and statistical tests to be used.

- ◆ There is a strong element of values, attitudes and judgements.

- ◆ It is locally based.

- ◆ It can be part of an individual or group project.

RETAIL CHANGE

Since the Second World War, the type and location of shops and shopping centres has changed. Some shops have moved from out of the town centres to shopping malls on the outskirts of urban areas to avoid congestion and high land prices. There has also been a shift away from privately-owned shops to nationally-owned chain stores. The 1960s saw a movement of the highest-order shops to pedestrianised precincts, causing a movement of the centre of towns towards these areas.

▶ Hypotheses

There are some interesting hypotheses relating to retail change, as follows.

◆ The number of low-order food shops has decreased over time.

◆ There has been an increase in the proportion of nationally-owned chain stores.

◆ Shops of similar functions will locate together and this tendency will increase over time.

◆ The most desirable location in the town will have changed due to pedestrianisation.

Fig. 6.47 Extract from a *Kelly's Directory*

▶ Data collection methods

◆ A historical study such as this draws much of its data from secondary sources. There are two main sources:
 – The **Kelly's** and **Marshalls'** **directories** which are available from the late 19th century. These give detail of the type and location of businesses.
 – The **GOAD maps** which show a shop's location, name and retail type. They can be purchased from the *GOAD* Map Shop. As they begin in 1969, they provide an important overlap with the directories.

◆ **Questionnaires** are a useful way of generating information from older residents and shopkeepers. Such an approach can give important supporting detail.

◆ A detailed **map** of present land use in the town could also be completed.

◆ **Old newspapers** and **archive photographs** can be used to illustrate changes.

HAMPSTEAD HIGH STREET

(N.W.3) (HAMPSTEAD). 1 Willoughby Road to 52 Heath Street. Map G3.

SOUTH-EAST SIDE
TRINITY
(PRESBYTERIAN CHURCH)

3   Pastry Ltd. bakers
4   High Hill Gallery. picture dlrs
5   Wright, Mrs K. ladies' outfitter
6   High Hill Bookshops Ltd. booksllrs
6a Colorcraft. screen process printers
6a Weaver, Sydney. photographer
6a Crane Atchison & Co. bookbinders
6b Mallock Leserve & Co. accntnts
7   Moores. grocers
8   Freeman, Hardy & Willis Ltd. boot mkrs
9   Metcalf, A.A. optician
9a Stowell F. S. Ltd. retail wine & spirit mers
10 King of Bohemia P. H.
12 Common Wealth
14 Page E. R. W. statnr
16 Hampstead Fisheries. fishmngrs

17 Lidstone Ltd. butchers
18 Davidson A. fruitr
19 New Era Laundry Co. Ltd
19a Lush & Cook Ltd. dyers & cleaners

   ... here is Gayton road ...

22 & 41 Bewlay (Tobacconists) Ltd
23 & 24 Crowe J. & Sons, funeral directors
25 & 26 Smith Rowland (Motors) Ltd. motor car dlrs
27 Knowles-Brown H. Ltd. jewellers
28a Harold Leighton. ladies' hairdrssr
28 Barclays Bank Ltd. (branch)
29 Stamp E. B. Ltd. chemists
30 Hampstead Foodfair Ltd. provision mers
30 Payne, Dyter & Son. bldrs
31 Feltone, ladies' outfitters
32 Hicks Richard (Provincial) Ltd. fruit mers
35 Anglo-Dutch Petroleum Co. Ltd
35 Blue Star Garages Ltd
35 Blue Star Properties Ltd. property owners
38 & 39 Bird-in-Hand P. H.

40 Fowler S. & Co. Ltd. domestic stores
40b Goy & Richards Ltd. estate agts
40c Universal Radiators Ltd. motor radiator reprs
41 & 22 Walker A. D. Ltd tobccnsts
42 Chicken Bar, restaurant

   .... here is Flask Walk ...

43 Maynards Ltd. confetnrs
44 Angerson Jas. Sydney, butcher
45 Cullen W. H. grocer
46 Lidington Jn. outfitter
47 Smith Harry, florist
Clark Derek H. & Co. Ltd, printers
Hampstead Underground Station

SOUTH-WEST SIDE
(from Heath Street)

55 National Provincial Bank Ltd
55 Norman Wm. L. dental surgu
56 Eastmans, dyers & cleaners
57 King H. S. statnr
58 Mac Fisheries Ltd. fishmngrs
59 Lipton Ltd. provsn. dirs
61 Aerated Bread Co. Ltd
62 Victoria Wine Co. Ltd
63 Hampstead BRANCH POST OFFICE

64 Tip Top Cleaners Ltd
64 Music Box, toy dirs

   ... here is Oriel Place ...

65/66 Gaze G. H. & Co. Ltd. drapers
67 Hampstead Bakery
68 & 69 Woolworth F. W. & Co. Ltd. bazaar
70 Mila. gowns
71 Riveria Restaurant
72 Skoyles F. J. & Co. radio & television receiving set dlrs

   ... here is Perrin's court ...

73 Forsters, grocers
74 Coffee Cup, cafe
76 Cook Sam (Fruiterers) Ltd. fruits

   ... here is Perrin's lane ...

77 King William IV P.H.
77, 78, 79, 80 & 81 Smith Rowland (Motors) Ltd
82 Green Hill Restaurant
82 Dorice Wools, wool shop
84 Willis Jas. & Son. Ltd. ironmongers

   ... here is Prince Arthur road ...

GREEN HILL (flats)
   1 Hoare J.F. physcn

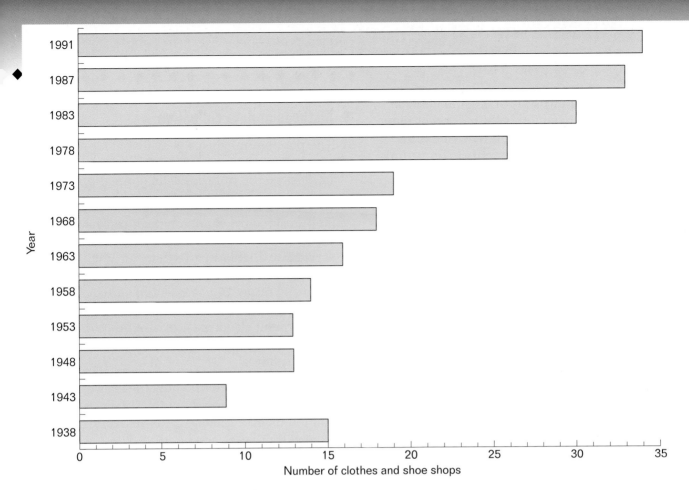

Fig. 6.48 The number of clothes and shoe shops

▶ Techniques

◆ To view the overall change in shop type and location, **base maps** should be used, perhaps showing five or more different street plans over the last 100 years.

◆ This can be followed up with **bar charts** and **line graphs** showing the increase or decrease in the number of different shop types over time.

◆ It is vital that as many **old** and **modern** **photographs** and **newspaper articles** are used to authenticate the maps and graphs.

◆ **Nearest neighbour index** (see page 56) can be used to describe whether shops are more clustered or less clustered today than they were in the past.

▶ Presentation

The beauty of this project is that the timescale allows for a number of different socioeconomic and historical trends to be linked to retail change.

Figure 6.48 gives an example of the type of change which can be depicted quite simply.

▶ Limitations of this project

◆ The project depends heavily on secondary data.

◆ If background evidence is missing (e.g. if *Kelly's* directories are difficult to obtain) then the project is weakened.

◆ The researcher must ensure that the investigation does not become a purely historical study – there must be a spatial element to the change.

▶ Strengths of this project

◆ Data collection is easy and readily available, once a local library archive has been located.

◆ Dependence on archive material means that the project is less subject to the vagaries of weather or public indifference.

◆ It is a relative inexpensive project, although *GOAD* maps and photocopying of maps and directories will mount up.

◆ Apart from the optional questionnaire, the enquiry can be completed quite safely without a partner.

7 Further geographical investigations

One of the major changes to rural settlements and small towns in the twentieth century is that they have become **suburbanised**. Increased mobility has allowed many small settlements to grow and develop as commuter settlements. In addition greater use of IT (the Internet and E-mail for example) will increasingly allow more people to live away from large towns and to work at home. Although many smaller settlements retain their charm, the residents are more 'urban' in their character and have little to do with farming, the original function of the settlement. This project investigates changes in rural settlements and small towns, in this case drawing on the experience of Woodstock.

▶ Topics to investigate

1 How has Woodstock increased in population over time?

2 To what extent is Woodstock a dormitory (or commuter) town?

3 How has the settlement grown, and what evidence is there for buildings of different ages?

4 How have the number and type of services in Woodstock changed over time?

▶ Methods of data collection

1 The population census is available for every 10 years since 1801 (except 1941) and can be found in most public libraries. The population size for each 10 years can easily be obtained.

2 'Kelly's Directories' are a type of census which provide information on the employment and services available in a settlement. It will not be necessary to examine copies for every year; a survey of every 20 years would suffice. The most recent census will show the current employment structure – or else this can be found out by using a questionnaire (to at least 30 households).

3 A building survey will show the ages of houses. Figures 7.1–7.4 show how the style of a building can tell us about its age. Alternatively, OS maps from earlier years can be used. These will show the size and shape of the settlement in previous times, which reveal changes when compared to current maps.

There are a variety of distinct housing types which relate to the period of development.

Fig. 7.1 Georgian town house

town houses often built in terraces

many chimney pots showing most rooms had a fireplace

steep slate roof, and large attic

drawing room or dining room on the first floor

bedrooms on second floor

reception rooms, library or study on the ground floor

large windows with small glass panes

fancy ironwork

kitchen, butlers pantry and wine cellar were 'below stairs' where servants were based

wide pavements

CHANGES IN SMALL SETTLEMENTS

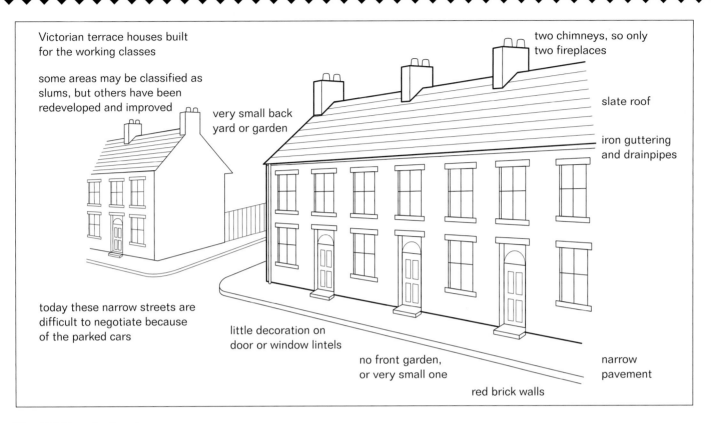

Victorian terrace houses built for the working classes

some areas may be classified as slums, but others have been redeveloped and improved

very small back yard or garden

two chimneys, so only two fireplaces

slate roof

iron guttering and drainpipes

today these narrow streets are difficult to negotiate because of the parked cars

little decoration on door or window lintels

no front garden, or very small one

narrow pavement

red brick walls

Fig. 7.2 Victorian housing

Fig. 7.3 Inter-war housing. Inter-war building was often poorly planned, and created ribbon development along roads leading out of towns. It looks like mile after mile of uniform housing, but there were open fields behind them. Post-war planners avoided ribbon development.

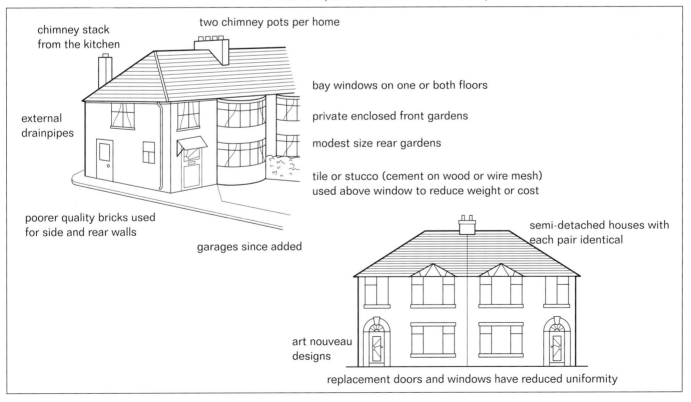

chimney stack from the kitchen

two chimney pots per home

bay windows on one or both floors

private enclosed front gardens

external drainpipes

modest size rear gardens

tile or stucco (cement on wood or wire mesh) used above window to reduce weight or cost

poorer quality bricks used for side and rear walls

garages since added

semi-detached houses with each pair identical

art nouveau designs

replacement doors and windows have reduced uniformity

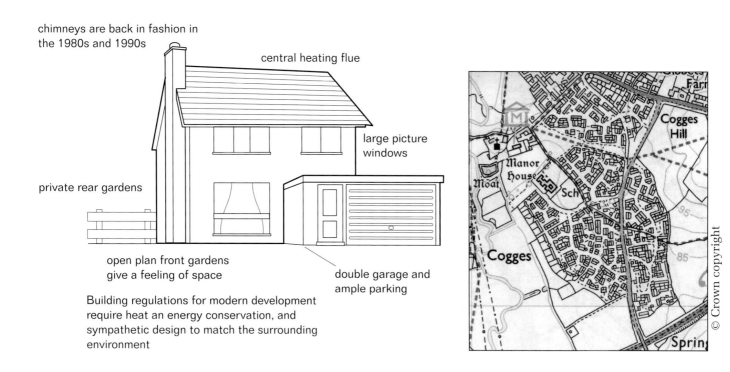

chimneys are back in fashion in
the 1980s and 1990s

central heating flue

large picture
windows

private rear gardens

open plan front gardens
give a feeling of space

double garage and
ample parking

Building regulations for modern development
require heat an energy conservation, and
sympathetic design to match the surrounding
environment

© Crown copyright

Fig. 7.4 Modern housing. The map shows a modern small private development. The houses are quite large and there is a fair degree of privacy provided by the street pattern. Few back gardens overlook each other. The development is set well back from a dual carriageway road.

The Georgian era of the 18th and early 19th centuries had a very grand style with Roman and Greek styles of architecture (Figure 7.1). In towns there are no front gardens, although iron railings mark the boundaries. Windows are large, although some were bricked in to avoid paying a window tax that the Government introduced in 1796. Often these houses have a cellar and in towns there may be three or more floors. Because these houses are large and central in the town they have often been taken over and used by businesses or shops.

Houses in the Victorian era were much smaller and often built in terraces (Figure 7.2). Improvements in transport made it easy to bring in materials from long distances, and houses used slate, iron and bricks. On a map we see the road network is very geometric or uniform and the housing is tightly packed. Houses built at the start of the 20th century, the Edwardian era of the 1900s to 1920s, were similar to Victorian housing

but larger; they also had larger windows, fancy brickwork and were built on larger plots of land.

Inter-war housing, largely built in the 1930s, is characterised by semi-detached and detached housing with bay windows, enclosed front and rear gardens, with many having their own garages (Figure 7.3). More recent housing, provided by private development, includes quite large detached houses with ample parking space (unlike Victorian housing which has none). They are often open-planned (lacking formal boundaries) with large private gardens at the rear (Figure 7.4). These developments are more common in small towns where land is available. By contrast new developments in urban areas are often at quite high densities.

▶ Techniques of presentation

1 A simple line graph will show how population has changed over time (Figure 7.5). Graphs should be annotated (labelled) to show periods of most rapid growth, slow growth and decline. Suggest reasons for such changes, such as the opening of a rail link, the building of a by-pass.

2 Pie charts or bar charts can be used to show changes in employment structure. If you can, draw proportional pie charts where the size of the whole pie is proportional to the working population of the settlement, while the divisions of the pie chart refer to the type of jobs people have.

3 A map can be drawn to show the size of the settlement at successive ages. In addition, photos can be taken to show representative buildings from each era. These should be labelled to show the main characteristics of the building (Figures 7.1–7.4).

4 The change in the number and type of services can be shown by line graphs (changes in functions over time) or proportional circles (the size proportional to the number of services available). These should be backed up with annotated photos – for example of a disused post office as shown in photo 6.1, see page 76.

▶ Strengths of the project

Increasingly more people are living in small settlements and rural settlements. A study of a person's home environment is an excellent way of getting to know the ins and outs of the local geography. In addition, this type of project can achieve very high marks because:

◆ it uses a variety of types of information, both primary and secondary

◆ it enables the student to use variety of techniques

◆ it allows first-hand observations, for example of building type, number of services, and use of questionnaires for occupation, place of work etc.

◆ it involves little danger or personal risk in completing the project.

▶ Limitations

All projects have their drawbacks. Studying changes in small settlements may cause problems because:

◆ all settlements are different: any conclusions drawn are place-specific

◆ updated OS maps are only available at irregular intervals

◆ smaller settlements might not show the variety of development stages that larger settlements show

◆ there is far more secondary than primary data

◆ depending on the settlement, it might be necessary to concentrate on one or two of the investigative topics suggested, rather than attempting them all.

Fig. 7.5 Population change in Woodstock 1801–1991

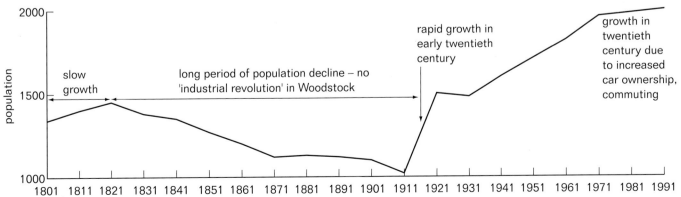

HYDROLOGY AND RIVER CHANNEL FIELDWORK

There are a number of aspects of rivers that we can investigate. While many books describe 'textbook' rivers (as on page 10) most rivers, especially those in lowland areas, have been influenced by human activity. Channels are straightened, new streams have been built for flood relief, and water is taken out of streams after being used for a variety of purposes. However, there are very important safety aspects in river fieldwork. You must not try to measure a river alone, or attempt to work on one that is too deep or too fast.

▶ Hypotheses

1 River characteristics (such as velocity, discharge, and bedload) change downstream.

2 The velocity of a river varies across a meander section.

3 Human activity has affected rivers in many ways.

▶ Techniques

◆ Cross-sections can be used to show variations in the river's width, depth and cross-sectional area.

◆ Flow-line maps (see page 42) are used to show changes in velocity downstream.

Fig. 7.6. The characteristics of upland and urban streams

Upland streams are characterised by:	Urban streams:
◆ steep slopes	◆ have a high sediment load, especially of silt
◆ small flood plains	◆ are slow moving
◆ a coarse bedload	◆ have banks overgrown with weeds
◆ many pools, ripples, boulders	◆ adjoin many polluting developments such as factories and sewage works which discharge into them
◆ high percentage of bare outcrop of rock	◆ have floodplains with housing, roads, railways, factories and other industries.
◆ high degree of roughness.	

◆ Spearman's Rank Correlation Coefficient (see page 54) can be used to test whether there is a relationship between distance from source and variables such as velocity or discharge.

◆ Dispersion diagrams (page 46) can be used to compare the bedload at one site with that at other sites.

◆ Annotated photos can be used to show particular site characteristics as well as the human impact on rivers.

▶ Data collection methods

Choose a *safe* river. It must be less than 1 metre deep, and you will be safer in one that is less than 75 cm. Access to the stream may be limited to places where footpaths border the river or where there are bridges. Most land next to rivers is privately owned, so you should ask for permission to use a particular stretch of water as the landowner will have rights over that section.

The river channel shape and cross-sectional area are measured by taking a number of readings.

◆ The **width** is found using a 20 metre tape measure. The river should be measured at normal flow and at bankfull flow (Figure 7.7).

◆ The **depth** of the river should be recorded every 50cm.

◆ The **cross-sectional area** is found by using the formula width × average depth, or more accurately by plotting the shape of the river on graph paper and then calculating its area.

◆ **Stream velocity** is measured with a flowmeter or with a floating object such as an orange. Friction with channel and bed sides will reduce velocity, so average velocity is found at 0.6 of total water depth.

If using a flowmeter:
– split the channel up into regular sections
– be sure to stand well downstream of the meter to reduce turbulence
– at each measuring point establish the velocity at a depth of 0.6 of the total depth.

Average velocity (aV) = $\Sigma V/n$ (where ΣV is the sum of the individual velocity readings and n = the number of readings taken)

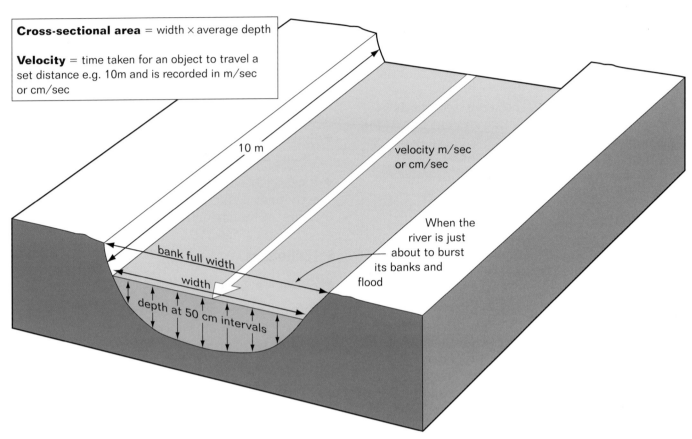

Cross-sectional area = width × average depth

Velocity = time taken for an object to travel a set distance e.g. 10m and is recorded in m/sec or cm/sec

10 m

velocity m/sec or cm/sec

When the river is just about to burst its banks and flood

bank full width

width

depth at 50 cm intervals

Fig. 7.7 Width, depth, CSA and velocity at normal and bankfull stages

When measuring velocity using a floating object (Figure 7.8):
– mark out a known length of channel (e.g. 10m)
– record the time taken for the orange to travel this distance
– repeat the process for greater accuracy
– repeat the process at intervals across the stream
– ignore readings where the orange or stick becomes caught by obstacles
– calculate the **average surface velocity** from these readings.

To obtain the average velocity from the average surface velocity use a multiplier of 0.8.

◆ The stream's **discharge** (Q) is the cross-sectional area (A) **×** average velocity (V).

◆ The stream's **load** helps us determine the work that a river is carrying out. The easiest measurement is that of bedload:
– at regular intervals across the channel going downstream remove a random sample of at least 30 bedload particles and record their diameter and length of longest side.

Fig. 7.8 Measuring velocity using an orange

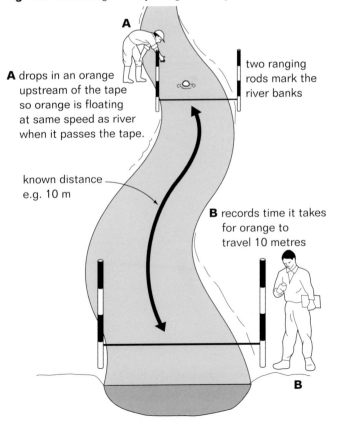

A

A drops in an orange upstream of the tape so orange is floating at same speed as river when it passes the tape.

two ranging rods mark the river banks

known distance e.g. 10 m

B records time it takes for orange to travel 10 metres

B

- The **meandering** in a river. The wavelength and amplitude of meanders are particularly interesting. To measure a meander:
  - use compasses to create a field sketch of the river's plan
  - measure the distance between two points by stream and by travelling in a straight line. If the distance by stream is greater by more than 1.5 times, the river is said to be sinuous (meandering); if it is more than four times the length it is highly sinuous (Figure 7.9)

It is also important to study the river from OS maps, especially 1:25 000 maps. We can work out the number of streams without tributaries (first order streams) and the number of streams of each subsequent order (Figure 7.10). This allows us to compare the stream network in the selected river basin with the theories of stream order. On some maps it may also be possible to study the meander pattern of a stream network or the impact of human activity on stream patterns (see for example the very straight pattern caused by the drainage ditches on page 21, in the south-western part of the map extract).

Fig. 7.9 Sinuosity and meandering in rivers

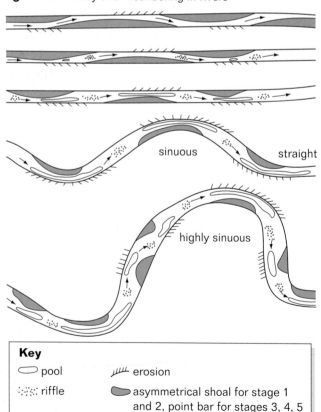

Key
- pool
- riffle
- erosion
- asymmetrical shoal for stage 1 and 2, point bar for stages 3, 4, 5

▶ Strengths of this project

- Most students have studied rivers as part of their geography course.
- Most parts of the country have many streams and rivers.
- Even streams which are heavily affected by human activity allow useful investigation.
- It can be used to show the impact of human activities on rivers as well as the impact of rivers on human activities.

▶ Limitations

- Rivers are dangerous, especially after floods.
- Any project investigating a river needs at least two people and for safety reasons ideally more than three.
- Rivers very enormously over the year, so the results in winter will be very different from those in summer. Indeed, there is a considerable difference before and after a storm.
- It is not always possible to gain access to the most promising part of a river.

Fig. 7.10 Stream order and OS maps

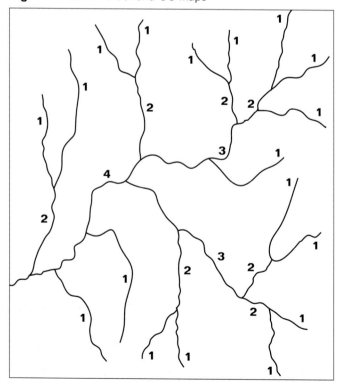

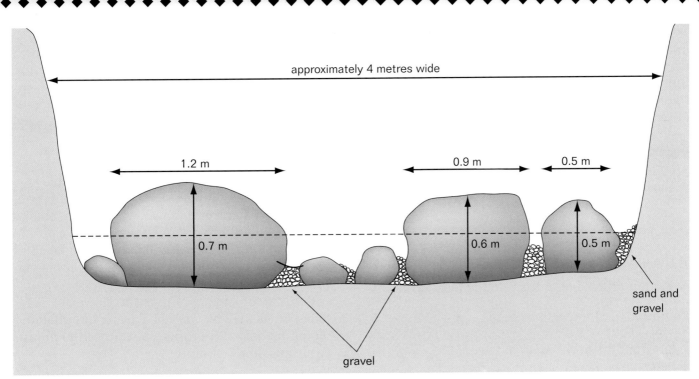

Fig. 7.11 Bedload: a mixture of boulders, stones and gravel

Fig. 7.12 Annotated photo of fieldwork methods

TOURISM AND RECREATION IN A SMALL TOWN

This project shows you how to investigate the impact of tourism or recreation or both on a small urban area. It can be adapted to look at the impacts in other types of tourist destination. The impacts of tourism include social, economic and environmental impacts. Social impacts include:

◆ the levels of irritation expressed by the host (local) population

◆ the nature and scale of problems caused by tourism and tourists.

Economic impacts include:

◆ the impact of tourism on small shopkeepers

◆ the importance of tourism to the local economy.

Environmental impacts include:

◆ overcrowding

◆ litter

◆ excess traffic.

▶ Hypotheses

◆ The distribution of tourist facilities is concentrated in selected areas.

◆ There are many positive impacts of tourism.

◆ Tourism also has negative impacts on the town.

◆ Most of the users are satisfied with the facilities and the attractions that are on offer.

▶ Methods

◆ A survey of the distribution of attractions and facilities related to tourism can be made by visiting all parts of the town to discover the attractions and facilities on offer. Alternatively it may be possible to obtain this data from Yellow Pages, Thompson's Directory, or the Tourist Information Centre.

◆ A questionnaire such as that in Figure 7.13 can be used to elicit the views of tourists, and one like Figure 7.14 for residents and those working in the tourist industry. You should interview at least 30 people from each group (30 is defined as the minimum number required for a large sample). It is important to obtain views from a number of different interest groups so as to have a balanced report. The questionnaire must be designed carefully and be preceded by a **pilot study** to assess its suitability. Vary the locations, days and times of day the questionnaire is used so as to achieve a representative cross-section of people. The results from tourists on a wet Tuesday in December will be very different from the results on a warm Sunday in August.

◆ Economic information is normally available from the local council. Many city centres now have a **City Centre Manager** who may be able to provide the information. All regions have a **Regional Tourist Board** which may also be able to provide economic data. In addition, it may be possible to interview specific businesses regarding the impact of tourism. However, companies may be wary of sharing information about income and profits, so you need to phrase your questions carefully.

◆ Environmental impacts can be assessed either by means of a questionnaire, an environmental survey, or through an environmental quality index. The latter involves a survey of the area and filling in a survey form (Figure 7.15). The survey should be supported with annotated photographs, labelled so as to make very clear the point you wish to make.

▶ Presentation of results

◆ A map showing the distribution of attractions and facilities is the best way to show what draws the tourists and what is provided for them. This can also be adapted for sports projects to show the distribution of parks, swimming pools, cinemas and so on. The type of recreational facility varies in each part of town (see Figure 7.17).

◆ The ease of access to the town can be shown using proportional circles (to show the number of car parking spaces and their distribution) and flow lines (the number of train and coach arrivals from selected destinations).

◆ The results from both questionnaires can be shown using bar charts, pie charts and pictograms. Where replies mention a particular point, e.g. litter, it is best to support this with an illustrative photo.

◆ The environmental quality survey can be shown using a bi-polar analysis (Figure 7.15).

Fig. 7.13 The impact of tourism: a simple questionnaire to tourists

Date, day and time . . . .

Location . . . .

Interviewee . . . .

Sex . . . . Ages of people in group . . . .

Where have you come from? . . . .

How did you get here? . . . .

What has attracted you to this place? . . . .

. . . .

What else are you going to visit? . . . .

. . . .

How long are you staying here? . . . .

What do you like about the attractions and the facilities for tourists here?

. . . .

. . . .

. . . .

Are there any disadvantages of this place?

. . . .

. . . .

. . . .

There are a number of advantages that tourism brings. How important do you think these advantages are?

	Very important	Quite important	Important	Unimportant
It creates many jobs				
It brings in a lot of money				
Local facilities are upgraded				
There are many spin-offs				

Any other advantages?

. . . .

Disadvantages of tourism

	Very important	Quite important	Important	Unimportant
Congestion, especially coaches				
Lack of parking				
Congested streets				
Too many tourists				
Language students				
Litter				
Pollution				

Are there any other disadvantages?

. . . .

. . . .

Overall do you think that tourism is a good thing for the town? . . . .

Fig. 7.14 Questionnaire for residents and those employed in the tourist industry

---

Location . . . .

Time . . . . Date . . . .

Best environment		1	2	3	4	5	6	7	8		Worst environment
No congestion											Very congested
No groups of people											Threatening 'gangs' of tourists
Quiet											Noisy
Clean streets											Polluted streets
Empty pavements											Congested pavements
Street furniture											None available
Many litter bins											No litter bins
Plenty of parking											No parking

Fig. 7.15 A simple bi-polar environmental survey

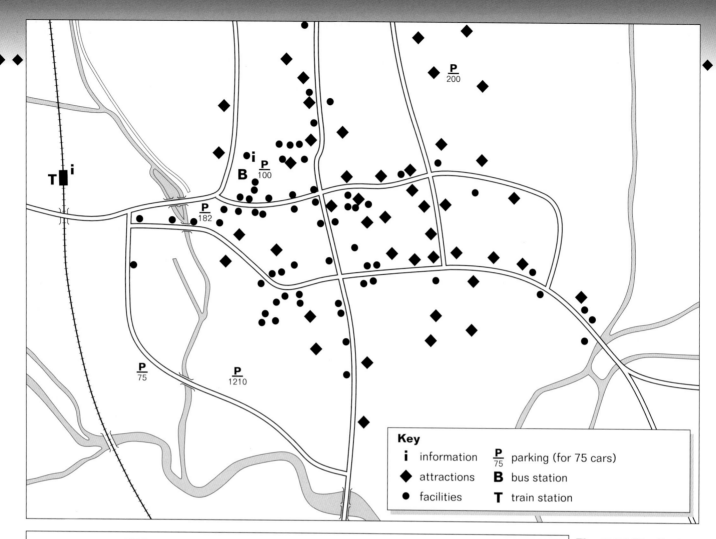

Key

i	information	$\frac{P}{75}$	parking (for 75 cars)
◆	attractions	**B**	bus station
●	facilities	**T**	train station

Fig. 7.16 Distribution of tourist-related facilities in a small town

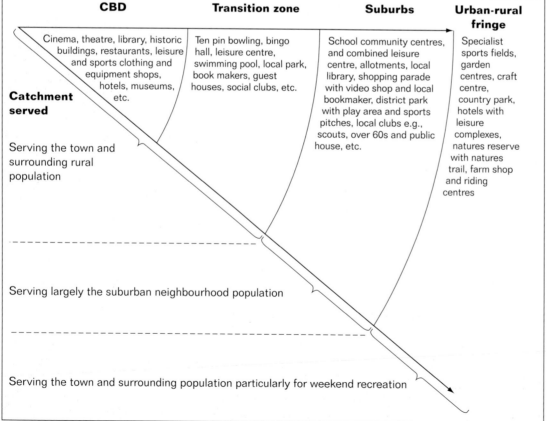

CBD	Transition zone	Suburbs	Urban-rural fringe
Cinema, theatre, library, historic buildings, restaurants, leisure and sports clothing and equipment shops, hotels, museums, etc.	Ten pin bowling, bingo hall, leisure centre, swimming pool, local park, book makers, guest houses, social clubs, etc.	School community centres, and combined leisure centre, allotments, local library, shopping parade with video shop and local bookmaker, district park with play area and sports pitches, local clubs e.g., scouts, over 60s and public house, etc.	Specialist sports fields, garden centres, craft centre, country park, hotels with leisure complexes, natures reserve with natures trail, farm shop and riding centres

Catchment served

Serving the town and surrounding rural population

Serving largely the suburban neighbourhood population

Serving the town and surrounding population particularly for weekend recreation

Fig. 7.17 Distribution of recreational related facilities in a small town

▶ Advantages of this project

◆ It is a very popular part of the syllabus.

◆ Tourism and recreation are increasingly important in society and are having an increasingly noticeable impact.

◆ It is a familiar field to many students who work in tourist facilities or take part in recreational activities.

◆ There is a wide variety of data available which lends itself to a variety of analytic techniques.

▶ Limitations of this project

◆ The results are very specific to the place and the time of study: results from surveys in spring and winter always include the weather as a disadvantage, whereas summer projects posit 'congestion' as the main problem.

◆ Information about economic impacts are at best imprecise.

Fig. 7.18 Promoting urban tourism

Fig. 7.19 The negative impact of tourism (overcrowding in a tourist honeypot)

USING THE CENSUS

A census is an official population count. In Britain, the census is carried out by the Office of Population Censuses and Surveys (OPCS). It has taken place every ten years since 1801 (except 1941 when the country was at war). The census not only counts the size of the population but also collects information on a range of economic and social variables such as family income, occupation (jobs), ownership or rental of house, long-term illness, overcrowding, ethnicity, and car ownership.

Most GCSE questions show information at a **county** or **regional** level. By contrast, most geographical enquiries look at information at the **ward** level or even at the level of **enumeration district**.

A **ward** is an administrative division of a town. Figure 7.20 shows the 18 wards which make up Oxford. By contrast, the enumeration districts are the smallest areas for which census data are available. They contain a handful of streets and have a population of about 500 people. Figure 7.21 shows the enumeration districts that form North

Questions

1 (**a**) On a copy of Figure 7.20 show the variations in unemployment in Oxford.
Make sure that you use no more than five groups such as 0.0-1.9%, 2.0-2.9%, 3.0-3.9% etc., or top three wards, next four, middle four, next four, bottom three.
(**b**) Describe the pattern that you have drawn (refer to maximum, minimum as well as patterns such as regular, random and clustered).

2 (**a**) Choose either car ownership or home ownership. Work out the percentage of car ownership or home ownership in each ward (car or home ownership/number of households × 100%).
(**b**) Plot the variations in the rate of car or home ownership.
(**c**) Describe the pattern that you have drawn.
(**d**) How does it compare with the map of unemployment?
(**e**) Suggest links between unemployment and car or home ownership, or say why you think there are none.

Fig. 7.20 Oxford city: wards

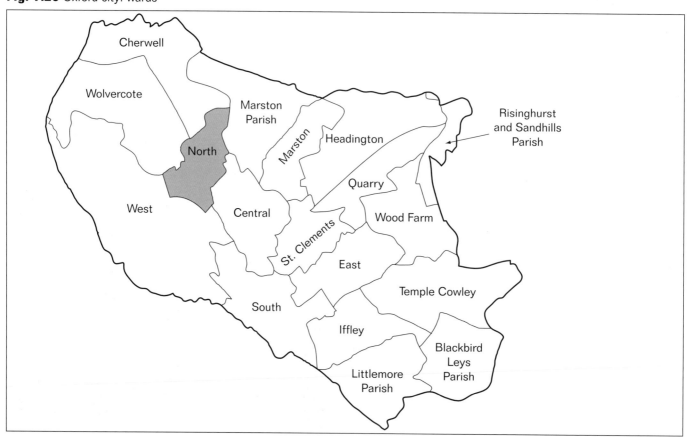

Ward in Oxford. Another scale, the district, is much larger, and may contain a city or a large rural population. Figure 7.22 shows the five districts that make up the county of Oxfordshire.

The information contained in the census is important for a number of reasons:

◆ it allows comparisons to be made

◆ it allows us to plan for the future. Variations in the birth rate, for example, will affect the number of schools that are needed in an area, while an ageing population creates demands for nursing homes, extra health care and pensions.

Figure 7.23 shows census data, at a ward level, for selected social and economic indicators for Oxford. A **household** refers to an individual or a group of people living at the same address with common housekeeping, such as sharing a living room, kitchen and so on. In this example the unemployed are those without a job. It does not include the **economically inactive** such as students, sick people, retired people and housewives.

Fig. 7.21 Enumeration districts in North Ward, Oxford

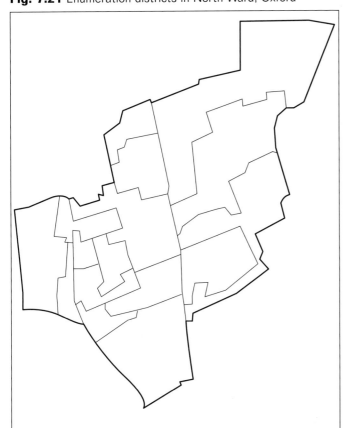

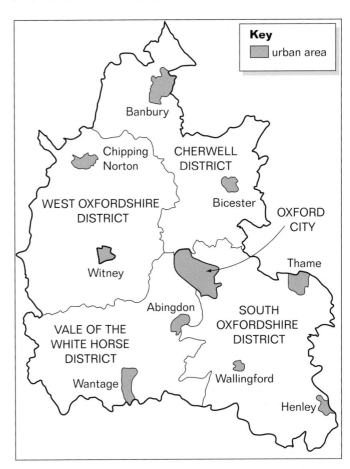

Fig. 7.22 Oxfordshire: districts

Fig. 7.23 Census data at ward level

	A	B	C	D
1	WARD	Households	Own house	Without car
2	Blackbird Leys	3039	133	1337
3	Central	286	0	154
4	Cherwell	2836	814	906
5	East Ward	2672	569	1079
6	Headington	2836	608	1018
7	Iffley	3106	1007	1164
8	Littlemore	2752	488	1098
9	Marston Parish	1263	477	273
10	Marston Ward	2512	626	820
11	North Ward	1947	435	753
12	Quarry Ward	2623	822	832
13	Risinghurst	1159	319	318
14	South Ward	2763	561	1304
15	St. Clements	3116	515	1447
16	Temple Cowley	2547	688	798
17	West Ward	2657	435	1315
18	Wolvercote	2867	967	875
19	Wood Farm	2711	613	916
20				

USING IT IN ENQUIRIES

Most students regularly use computers. In geography, computers offer us many useful features such as:

◆ word processing

◆ cartographic methods

◆ presenting data in a graphical form

◆ statistical packages

◆ spreadsheets

◆ satellite images

◆ CD Roms

◆ access to the Internet.

One of the great strengths of computers is the speed with which they operate. In addition, they have huge memory stores and make large amounts of information readily available. But it is important that we remember that computers are only a tool. Once we have the information or the image we must assess and explain it in a geographical way. Examiners are not testing students on computing knowledge but on knowledge of geography.

Most geography students use computers for their personal enquiries or projects. There are many advantages in this. First, a project that is word processed can look much better than one which is handwritten. More importantly, it is easier to edit mistakes on a computer than in a handwritten project. Second, spreadsheets allow us to make

calculations very easily. The example of a spreadsheet on (Figure 7.24) shows this clearly. Imagine how long it would take to work out the answer using a calculator. Third, computers give us a range of graphical techniques including cartographic (map) graphics. It may take time to learn the correct procedures on the computer but once you have mastered them you progress very fast.

The usefulness of the computer really depends upon the person using it. The computer is a machine that will only do as it is told. It is vital that you plan your work on the computer just as you plan your work on paper. Think about your aims. What is the purpose of using the computer? What are you trying to achieve? Find out about the packages (software) that are available and choose the most appropriate for your task.

Finally, make sure that you keep a back-up copy of all the work you do. Too many people who lose their work fail to have a copy of what they have done. It only takes moments to back up even quite large documents, but weeks or months to do all the work again.

▶ Using spreadsheets

Much of the work for statistics can be done by using spreadsheets. Although the specific details vary from program to program, there are a number of generalisations which are true for most spreadsheet software.

	B	C	D	E	F	G	H
1	Adult Pop.	UNEMPLOYED	Percentage	Households	White	Afro-Caribbean	Asian
2	6202	594	9.58%	3039	2763	235	18
3	474	11	2.32%	286	262	2	11
4	5240	211	4.03%	2836	2688	34	35
5	5283	363	6.87%	2672	2370	80	152
6	5721	335	5.86%	2836	2733	68	26
7	6093	315	5.17%	3106	2947	63	67
8	5531	319	5.77%	2752	2639	51	37
9	2796	115	4.11%	1263	1289	8	11
10	5023	194	3.86%	2512	2386	30	47
11	3545	122	3.44%	1947	1851	9	19
12	5136	222	4.32%	2623	2505	30	33
13	2316	99	4.27%	1159	1118	15	6
14	5234	348	6.65%	2763	2589	62	112
15	5918	473	7.99%	3116	2746	86	190
16	5288	289	5.47%	2547	2350	84	76
17	4601	254	5.52%	2657	2512	35	56
18	5262	201	3.82%	2867	2717	29	33
19	5517	277	5.02%	2711	2591	52	28
20	85180	4742	5.57%	Data in columns D to K refer to households not individuals			
21							
22			1 To find percent unemployment type =C2/B2				
23			2 Then Fill down				

Fig. 7.24 Spreadsheet

Question

1 Using Figure 7.24 work out the percentage of white, Afro-Caribbean and Indian people in each of Oxford's wards. Follow the instructions to work out a percentage and then fill the column.

1 On the hard disk enter into your spreadsheet program.

2 You should be facing a screen with lots of blank rows and columns on it. Fill the labels into the first row and column. Then enter the data into the adjacent rows and columns e.g. Figure 7.24.

3 The spreadsheet allows us to enter formulae into boxes (cells) which will then compute the answer using the data we have already put in.

The following formulae are very useful:
to find the sum, type **= Sum (B1..B18)**
to find the average, type **= Sum (B1..B18)/18**
to multiply two values (such as B1 multiplied by C1), type **= B1*C1**
to divide one value by another (such as B1 divided by C1), type **= B1/C1**
to find the standard deviation, type **= STDEV (B1..B18)**
to find the square root (for example of cell B1), type **= (B1 ^ 0.5)**
to find the square of a box (for example of cell B1), type **= B1*B1**

Typing '=' alerts the computer that what follows is a formula rather than a value. Once you press Return or click the tick on screen the result will be automatically presented.

There is no need to type the formula into all the cells in a row or a column. To transfer the formula to all the boxes in that row or column:
1 click on the cell containing the formula

2 holding the mouse down, drag across the row or column to select all the boxes

3 on the Calculate menu choose Fill Right or Fill Down as appropriate.

Another useful function is that of sorting data into ascending or descending order, using the Sort function:
1 highlight the data that you wish to sort

2 choose the Calculate mode on the menu

3 enter the boxes to be sorted (starting with the top left and finishing with the bottom right e.g. B2..C8)

4 choose whether you wish them to be in ascending or descending order and based on whichever key e.g. if the columns contained names and marks you could have them alphabetically or in descending order of marks.

▶ The Internet

The internet is a world-wide network of computers which allows users to gain information from organisations and individuals, as well as allowing users to communicate with them directly electronically. Electronic Mail or E-mail allows people to send messages via a computer modem and telephone lines to another person or organisation anywhere in the world (as long as they are connected to the internet and a phone line).

The internet is an extremely useful tool for geographers. There can be frustrations, however, as new web sites appear and others close. There is an increasing number of very large sites which are rather like encyclopaedias.

Finding information on the net
The internet allows us to:
◆ find information which is not available through books or newspapers

◆ 'talk' directly to other people: to ask questions, swap ideas and information

◆ update information.

A **search engine** is a website which allows a user to enter a key word or phrase in order to search for information which is then displayed on the screen. The **home page** is the first page on a website. It acts as a signpost or menu for the website.

Before you start, have a clear structure, timetable and goal. Have specific questions around an idea or issue that you wish to have answered. Once you have the information you need, you still have to use it wisely and know how to communicate the results.

Try out some websites. What can the following sites tell us, for example, about the state of the world's population and its use of resources? Alternatively, find out the location of the last earthquake to have occurred: where and when was it, how strong, what was its impact?

www.geog.le.ac.uk/cti
www.rgs.org
www.geography.org.uk
www.thornes.co.uk
www.stedwards.oxford

GLOSSARY

accessibility – a measure of how easy it is to reach a place. It can be measured by the number of bus routes that go to a place, or the number and type of roads, or the number of parking spaces available.

aerobic respiration – breathing by living organisms who use oxygen from the surroundings and give out carbon dioxide and water.

annotation – notes or comments added as explanation to a photograph or sketch map.

arête – a steep-sided, knife-edged ridge separating two cirques.

auger – a tool with the end shaped like a screw, for boring holes in the ground to take soil samples.

bar – a ridge of sediment which is parallel to the coast.

bay – a sheltered indentation in a coast, between two headlands.

bedrock – the solid unweathered rock that lies beneath the loose surface deposits.

bibliography – a list of all books, articles, Internet sites and any published material used in an enquiry.

biotic index – a list of plant and animal species (usually linked to illustration) for identification in the field.

blow out – an area within a sand dune system where bare sand has been removed by strong winds.

break-of-slope – the point at which the gradient of a point shows a marked change.

central place theory – a theory explaining the number, location, size, spacing and functions of a settlement.

centrality – see 'accessibility'.

cirque/corrie – a semi-circular steep-sided basin cut into the side of the mountain by a glacier.

climax vegetation – vegetation in a stable balance with the climate and soils of an area.

clinometer – an instrument used to measure slope angle.

commuter – a person who travels regularly between home and workplace.

corrie – see 'cirque'.

cruciform – a term used to describe settlements shaped like a cross.

dispersed settlement – a rural settlement pattern where most people live in scattered farmsteads.

dormitory town – a town with many residents but few services; also called a commuter town.

drainage basin – all the rain that falls over a drainage basin feeds the stream or river system of that basin.

drumlin – a glacial deposit of a low hummocky nature.

easting – a longitudinal gridline.

Edwardian – 1900s-1920s: houses are similar to Victorian but larger and more ornate.

enumeration districts – the name given to the smallest division of the UK's census small area statistics; an enumeration district is a subdivision of a ward.

escarpment – a long, continuous, steep-slope face of a ridge or plateau, usually associated with tilted rocks.

esker – a glacial deposit of gravel and sand which forms a steep-sided ridge that winds across an area.

estuary – the widening channel of a river where it nears the sea with a mixing of fresh water and salt (tidal) water.

ethnic minorities – an immigrant or racial group regarded as a distinct cultural body.

eutrophication – a process by which pollution (from sources such as sewage or fertilised fields) causes rivers and ponds to become over-rich in organic and mineral nutrients, so that algae and surface plants grow quickly and deplete oxygen.

evaluation – an awareness of the limits of a study, balancing the positive against the negative aspects of methods, results and conclusions.

externality – a factor that cannot be changed by an individual, e.g. accessibility or air pollution.

floodplain – the flat area bordering a river, composed of sediment deposited by floods.

Georgian – 18th–19th century; housing is characterised by Greek and Roman architecture.

gentrification – the process by which residential areas are improved and upgraded by individual owners and local authorities.

gulleying – the action of heavy rainwater on slopes whereby channels or small valleys are eroded.

hanging valley – a tributary valley entering a main valley at a much higher level because of over-deepening of the main valley, especially by glacial erosion.

headland – a narrow area of land jutting out into the sea.

hierarchy – a system which arranges things in graded or ranked order.

high-order goods – expensive goods such as cars, televisions and furniture. People are prepared to shop around for the best bargains.

home page – the first page on a website: it is a signpost or menu for a website.

impermeable – a solid which does not allow water to pass through it.

interlocking spurs – projections of high land which a river in its upper course is forced to wind around.

linear settlement – a settlement which has a long and narrow shape, associated with a road or valley bottom.

longshore drift – a process whereby beach material is gradually shifted laterally along the beach as a result of waves breaking diagonally.

low-order goods – everyday goods such as bread, milk and newspapers. People do not travel far or shop around for bargains.

meander – a curve or bend in a river.

moraine – a mass of rock and sand carried by a glacier and forming ridges and mounds when deposited (see 'drumlins' and 'eskers').

multiplier effect – a process whereby a change (e.g. location of a new industry) sets in a chain reaction of further growth.

northing – a latitudinal grid line.

nucleated settlement – a rural settlement which involves hamlets and villages of closely packed homes and farmsteads.

permeable – a solid which allows water to pass through it.

pilot study – a trial study assessing the validity of an enquiry and gauging improvements that need to be made.

primary data – is data that collected firsthand. It includes all fieldwork, observations, questionnaires and surveys.

pyramidal peak – a sharp peak formed where arêtes separating three or more cirques intersect.

range – refers to the maximum distance that people are prepared to travel for a good or service.

ribbon lake – a long, relatively thin lake forming in the bottom of a glaciated valley.

scale – the ratio between the actual size and map size of an area; scale is shown by a representative fraction and a scale line.

secondary data – includes all secondhand or published information such as the census, published data, articles, reports, books, maps and statistics.

search engine – a website where you enter a key word or phrase to search for information which is then displayed on screen.

socioeconomic – relating to both social and economic factors.

soil organic content – the amount of dead plant and animal material in the soil.

sphere of influence – the area that a settlement serves. The spere of influence of a town is much greater than that of a village or a hamlet.

spit – a low, narrow ridge of pebbles or sand, joined to the coastline at one end with the other end terminating in the sea; it is formed by longshore drift.

threshold – the minimum number of people required to keep a service going.

tombolo – when a bar joins a island to the mainland.

trickle down – is the only process by which benefits, such as economic growth, occur in smaller settlements having previously only been found in larger places.

Victorian – late 19th–early 20th century; characterised by small, terraced housing.

ward – an administrative division of a town, generally comprising a handful of streets: about 500 people.

INDEX